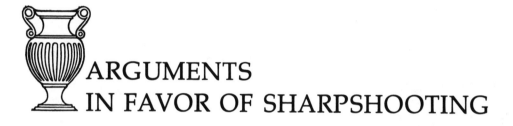

ARGUMENTS IN FAVOR OF SHARPSHOOTING

ARGUMENTS IN FAVOR OF SHARPSHOOTING

David Clarke

TIMBER PRESS
Portland, Oregon
1984

TIMBER PRESS
P.O. Box 1631
Beaverton, Oregon 97075

To the Teachers:
    Richard Thiel
    Julius Weinburg
    William Kleinsasser
    Derek deSolla Price

Students of man's various dimensions—government, society, economy, institutions—traditionally assume their subject matter to be accessible to full rational understanding. Indeed, they aim at finding "laws" capable of scientific proof. Human action, however, they tend to treat as nonrational, that is, as determined by outside forces, such as their "laws." The political ecologist, by contrast, assumes that his subject matter is far too complex ever to be fully understood—just as his counterpart, the natural ecologist, assumes this in respect to the natural environment. But precisely for this reason the political ecologist will demand—like his counterpart in the natural sciences—responsible actions from man and accountability of the individual for the consequences, intended or otherwise, of his actions.

Peter F. Drucker
Preface, *Men, Ideas and Politics,* 1971.

Contents

Author's Notes   1

Foreword by John Cheever   7

Chapter I
   Design in General   11

Chapter II
   The Rise of Empiricism in Architecture   27
      Part One: To World War II   27
      Part Two: World War II and After   35
      Part Three: Science, Technology, Education
         and Society   44
      Part Four: The Three Waves in Architecture   65

Chapter III
   Towers   91

Chapter IV
   Being Between Dogma   103

Chapter V
   Ordinary People   111

Chapter VI
   Environmental Disassociation   119

References   131

Proper Name and Citation Index   133

Author's Notes

There has been continuous breast-beating, both here and, say, Europe, for the last fifteen years about the "crisis" in architecture. One point I hope I've made in this book is that architecture is not alone; the proper set of the afflicted is in fact the professions, of which architecture is but one. The intent of this revelation is not to offer consolation, but to aid in seeking the *essence* of the problem. Common problems are strong clues and if we will use what we have left of our various professional methods to heal ourselves, there will be reason for optimism regarding our future ability to help others. Another point has been to try to do this beating of the breast as little as possible in favor of finding genuine ways out of our now very diffused difficulties. Thus I join the extremely youthful tradition perhaps started by William Hubbard's *Complicity and Conviction* (1981). There are now enough books on the failure of architecture. It is time to start laying foundations instead.

What do we mean by "sharpshooting"? The long answer is the subject of this book, pursued through the case study of architecture and one person's growing perceptions. Other cases will hopefully follow in other professions. The short, and thus defective, answer is that sharpshooting is a special subset of "problem-solving", a phrase that has lost much of its value in recent decades as droves of self-purported problem solvers solved problems that tended to come unstuck in unendearing short spaces of time. The true sharpshooter is careful to neither over or undersolve problems. This is a salient characteristic. First of all an oversolved problem is sure to be more expensive than it otherwise would be. Secondly, an undersolved problem will also be more expensive, if for no other reason than because some part of the problem is still there and nagging. It can also be deadly, as in undersolved structural design or nuclear holocaust strategic gaming. One characteristic of *both* under and oversolved problems is that they seem to almost always generate wicked side-effects. Also, it is exceedingly common that if a problem is oversolved in one area it will be undersolved in another. This is the syndrome of creating more errors to neutralize, balance out or cover up errors already made. In architecture one thinks of Robert Venturi's well-known house for his mother. First it was designed, as a manifesto, to contain global rather than local meaning (oversolved). That error was compounded by using very cheap materials and construction (undersolved), the enormity of it all supposedly made inoffensive by a patina of wit. But the problems don't cancel, being in different categories, and instead accumulate. Mrs. Venturi has been as silent as one would hope a mother would be on such an issue but when Mies van der Rohe did much the same thing in reverse, without the wit, for a hapless doctor named Farnsworth in Plano, Illinois fifteen years earlier it ended up in court. Indeed, being an expert witness in architecture cases these days is a tenable pastime. In related arenas one thinks of a $100,000 research project to see if people like windows in buildings. A trip to the library to see if there has ever been a sustained period or culture in history that has done without them would have sufficed.

Another characteristic is that the sharpshooter doesn't leave part of a problem unsolved just because his or her favorite tools happen not to be fashioned expressly for that purpose. Nor does the sharpshooter manufacture a "problem" for no other reason than because he or she has some tools lying around that are fulfilling to use. In most cases these days the parts of problems that do not get solved and thus nag on happen to be the ones that do not firm up empirically; that is, cannot be neatly expressed and disposed of through impersonal algorithms. Our sharpshooter uses a hammer to nail nails but prefers a whisk for making mayonnaise. Since our empiricist problem solver realizes that he or she will look foolish sticking his or her beloved hammer in the eggs, this sort normally prefers to claim that the state of being without mayonnaise is not a problem—even if society claims in a single voice that it is. This is the second theme of the book.

The third theme of the book, peculiar to architecture as a point but not as a type, is ornamentation; partly because the issue is so blatant these days but mostly because it crystallizes so well the problem of the empiricists. Attention is drawn to Eliel Saarinen and Louis Sullivan, the last known architects to do really competent

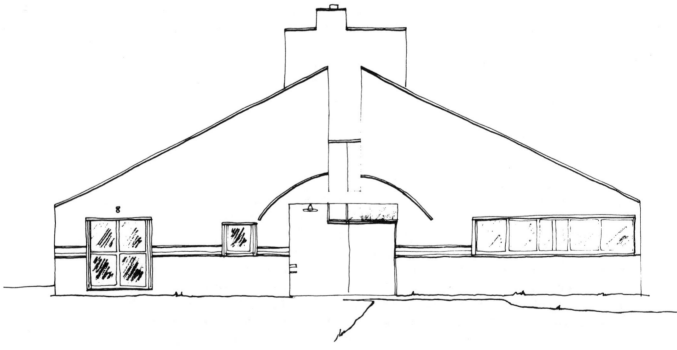

Architecture as *angst:* aged widow Vanna Venturi's 1962 house by her son. Cardboard zips and zaps reflect 20th century existential miasma, including tortured stairs, for a woman likely seeking peace, quiet, and no stairs at all.

ornament and to simultaneously claim without contradiction that their forms followed function. Ornament became the mayonnaise of architecture and the worst joke of the year is that, finally forced to recognize the problem, empiricist-type problem solvers have brought to market computer graphic software that work as electronic ornament templates. In other words, they finally stuck the hammer in the eggs. The sharpshooter is both laughing and crying.

The fourth theme of the book, as a persistent undercurrent, has to do with ethics. In preferring process to product and algorithms to personally accountable decision-making one is committing a special case of Aristotle's "appeal to authority" fallacy. This is exactly the social satire aimed at the Wizard of Oz: a man-made being conjured for the express purpose of acquiring more authority than the man would alone. The process, algorithm, program or Wizard is supposed to have its own ability to seek truth and even have a sense of fair play; it never does, save for what its designers give it. Yet few think clearly enough to see that the designers are not only responsible for the system but also for its decisions. Indeed, it's far too common that our leaders and executives, wishing a decision they know is unacceptable, will work backwards from it to a process they know will "impersonally" generate it. More benignly, but just as dangerously, the system designer often simply leaves to take another job, leaving his or her alter ego-system behind, which no one knows how to drive and which soon careens wildly out of control.

The fifth theme, perhaps the least sure but nevertheless the one that integrates the others, is relentless speculation on the economic winding down of the West. We now know that the Middle Ages was a period of continual technological effervescence. It took us a while to find this out because they *made* technological advances rather than *theorized* (i.e., published) about them. Relatively speaking,

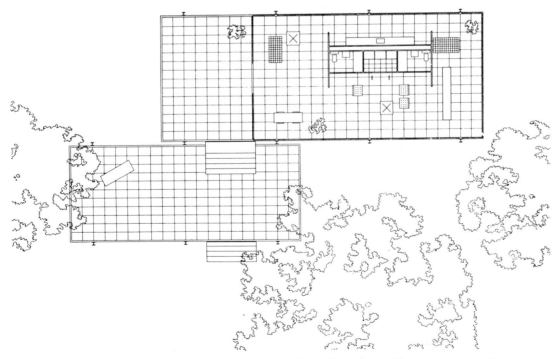

Architecture as scientific reduction: Mies van der Rohe's glassy box with no screens or air conditioning in the land of brutal winters and torrid summers and many, many mosquitos. Client Farnsworth sued.

4 the Renaissance was a period of technological slow-down but what technology there was was very well documented (i.e., published). That theorizing, publishing, and documenting was paid for out of capital accumulated during the late Middle Ages. We are in a similiar "Renaissance" today (note the epiphenomenal "Ren Cen" in beautiful downtown Detroit) being paid for out of capital accumulated during our industrial age. Unfortunately, the money is not only now gone but we have heavily borrowed against an uncertain future to continue financing the party. The book argues that it's time to go back to work. Indeed, throughout 1984 we have been looking for evidence of the wrong book. It is not George Orwell who has correctly predicted the future but rather Herman Hesse in his *Magister Ludi: The Glass Bead Game* (1943):

> "At various times the Game was taken up and imitated by all the scientific and scholarly disciplines, that is, adapted to the special fields. There is documented evidence for its applications to the fields of Classical philology and logic. The analytical study of musical values has lead to the reduction of musical events to physical and mathematical formulas. Soon afterward philology borrowed this method and began to measure linguistic configurations as physics measures processes in nature. The visual arts soon followed suit, architecture having already led the way in establishing the links between visual art and mathematics."

The point is not that an isolated canker has spring up in the field of architecture but that it has slowly and inexorably moved through the whole body of thinking society. Like frogs in a slowly heated pan of water, no one could precise the point when they should jump, so no one did. The professions are being infected last, in fact, and their resistance thus far has been admirable testimony to their resilience and capacity to endure. There are now whole sectors of Western societies who are, in the medium term, engaged in essentially non-productive pursuits at direct or indirect public expense. This expense is borne by cadres of journeymen and professionals who's ability to produce the necessary wealth is more and more compromised. Since they can never cover the full cost much of it is borrowed against a future that is more and more likely to be profitless.

In structure, the book is a *bildungsroman,* in reverse order. It starts at the rear, with my being soapy but curious and ends, at the front, with my being less confused but certainly not yet wholly enlightened. It is, as well, a *bildungsroman* not just of one person but of a certain generation of professionals. There is little that has been unique about my progress.

John Cheever originally wrote the Introduction, at my request as Executive Editor, for a special issue of the *Journal of Architectural Education* (Volume XXX, Number 2), whose theme was architectural preservation. In his letter of transmittal, now in the ACSA files, John advised me that I could do anything I wanted with it. Both earlier and later, on Cedar Lane in Ossining, we spoke of other projects, such as a book of readings revealing acuity of place. Along with the Russians, Hugo and Hardy, John had a fantastic sense of place. John was being disingenuous about not qualifying as an amateur architect, as Marcel Breuer, Max Abramovitz and every architect worth knowing in Ossining and Fairfield County, Connecticut, well knew.

Chapter I was originally published as "Design Training" in *How It Works,* copyrighted by Marshall Cavendish House of London in the middle-late seventies. It is reprinted here with their kind permission even though it is greatly altered. You won't find the chapter in the American edition as the wrap editors thought it too difficult for American eighteen year olds. Thanks to Cathy Thomas of the FAA/DOT for the Dulles plan and to Angel Biasatti of the Dallas/Fort Worth airport for that plan. Thanks to Tim Healy of Krueger in Green Bay for the technical drawing of the Vertebra chair. The Musée Pompidou line shot is reprinted courtesy of Simon Bargate of the Hamlyn Group in London, original publishers of the *Anatomy of Architecture,* where you will find it in gorgeous color. Thanks to Moshe Safdie for Jerry Spearman's photo of Habitat.

Chapter II owes a great deal to several people. Highest on the list is Allen Rosenstein of UCLA's School of Engineering, whom I met as a co-panelist at a NSF/UCLA conference on the role of the humanities in undergraduate teaching in the late seventies (it was at this conference that I heard Ken Boulding describe the U. S. as a "grants economy"). Allen and I both presented papers coming to remarkably similar conclusions from totally different sets of experiences. So long as I was in Washington we continued to meet over the years and each time I was immeasurably enriched. Finally, I realized that to proceed in this direction I needed more formal study in economics, so I dropped out for three years from 1979 to 1981 and got some. It did nothing to improve on Allen's analysis of the dynamic situation we are in, for which I have merely acted as an amanuensis. Allen has several books inside himself ready to be dictated but he is too busy writing legislation for the more perceptive and far-seeing of our national legislators to sit down and do it. If I have to choose between Allen's laws and a book I'll take the laws any day, but I hope we get both. While the Chapter has gone through substantial revision and extension I should like to add that it began in 1963 as an undergraduate paper at Wisconsin for Julius Weinberg under the title "Logical Positivism and Social Value". Thanks also to Stephen Dresch of the Center for Demographic Studies in New Haven for inspiration; the same to Yale's Derek deSolla Price. Special thanks also to the University of Washington's Phil Thiel and the University of Wisconsin/Milwaukee Environment-Behavior Institute's Gary T. Moore for reading and commenting on parts of the typescript. For both Phil and Gary this was an emotion-charged task that they discharged, as we often say but seldom mean, as gentlemen and scholars. Special thanks too to Aristide Esser for his close reading and keen suggestions. For this chapter as well as the rest, I should add, being a great help doesn't mean agreeing with any of it whatsoever. The tesserae illustration is reprinted with the permission of the author and is from Derek deSolla Price's "The Development and Structure of the Biomedical Literature" in *Coping With the Biomedical Literature: A Primer for the Scientist and Clinician,* edited by Kenneth S. Warren and published in 1981. The Pullman worker housing is from a drawing by Klaus Kretschmann in 1976 and is reprinted with permission from the Historic Pullman Foundation in Chicago, to which I recommend a visit. The Linz Café drawings are courtesy of *Architectural Design* magazine. The Villa Wittgenstein is from Bernhard Leitner's *The Architecture of Ludwig Wittgenstein,* 1973, and is reprinted courtesy of the copyright holders, the Press of the Nova Scotia College of Art and Design and the New York University Press. Thanks to *Werk* for the van Eyck photos from their January 1962 issue. And to David English of the NSF for government spending figures. Finally, it should be noted that Chapter II was given informally at the 1983 Annual Meeting of the Society for General Systems Research on the invitation of the "Ecology of Knowledge" group and that another version of it was published by ASMER as a monograph in 1984.

"Towers" previously appeared in both *Gargoyle,* a copyright-free literary magazine and subsequently, under the pen-name of J. Wraith, in Brink Jackson's special issue of the *JAE,* Volume XXX, Number 1 in 1976.

6

"Between Dogma" was first presented as a lecture at Cranbrook Academy on the occasion of a national faculty seminar in architecture sponsored by the ACSA and AIA in the middle seventies. Special thanks to New York's Gerry Allen for continuing to encourage me all these years to publish it. Susan Waller ably assisted in finding Cranbrook photos to match the concepts. The photos were finally purchased from the Cranbrook Academy of Art/Museum.

"Environmental Disassociation" was written in 1967 and first presented at a conference sponsored by the University of Kentucky in 1970. As a lecture it has been to Yale, Oregon, Cal/Berkeley, CCNY and other places. It is presented here in abbreviated form with the original references.* Its *raison d'être*, dating back to 1965, was to persuade the faculty at the University of Oregon to permit me to put decoration in my design work, pure heresy at the time.

Other illustrations were somehow made by me, except for the graphs, for which I thank Frank Cycenas.

Special thanks to Linda Patrick, her faithful crew and her IBM Display Writer.

---

*Which are thus excluded from the general index except for proper names.

Foreword

by John Cheever

THE SECOND MOST EXALTED OF THE ARTS

Speaking as a novelist, and as a novelist who insists that the principal canon of aesthetics is communication, I am sometimes inclined to put architecture at the head of the list; but since my own profession is seriously imperiled—and has been for centuries—self-esteem and loyalty to my vocation demand that I put the Art of Fiction above architecture. I have no knowledge of architecture—indeed, would not qualify as an amateur—but I live in houses, worship in churches, attend events in auditoriums and sports arenas and, finding myself in countries where I can neither speak nor read the language, I count much more on architecture than on any other means of communication to speak to me succinctly of the remote past, the immediate past and the present aspiration of a people to whom I can barely say "good morning". I spent a summer recently in Roumania where no language that I speak was understood. I counted on the architecture of that country for the only fluent and profound conversation that was available to me and the eloquence of Dragomirna, the stone farmhouses and log cabins in Moldavia, the war ruins, the ghastly monuments of the Iron Guard and Anna Pauker's cruel and tragic attempt to Stalinize that nation were all more emphatically narrated by the buildings I saw than by any of the translated poetry, fiction or history that I read.

If architecture is not the most exalted of the arts it is surely the most naked. Even a poet can dissemble an iconoclastic sexual career but it seems to me that I can, in a building, read the timbre and structure of the architect's intelligence, his dates, the universities he has attended, his digestive tract, his bank balance and his competence at dealing with other men and women. Wit and intelligence shine in a facade. So do obesity, drunkenness and prejudice. Anyone can guess Stanford White's height and Richardson's girth; and from one look at the Kaufmann house in Pennsylvania I knew Frank Lloyd Wright's shoe-size. Poets can put on false beards and smuggle their forbidden manuscripts across policed borders but an architect's passion for his time, his place and the native raw materials of his craft produce few facile emigrants. One of the greatnesses of architecture is its expression of the imponderables—the visionary or spiritual aspects of our natures—and thus its detestation of despotism. A rich mixture of courage, intelligence and inspiration is demanded. One finds it oftener in the novelist, of course, but one occasionally finds it in architects. If we are comfortable and happy we are not always accountable for the degree of corruption around us. When one is in doubt one has only to ask what is being built.

I live in one of the provincial environs of New York City where the conversion of large estates into tracts of small houses is the principal architectural activity. The costs of construction quite naturally determine the character of these communities but there are some displays of taste. The most successful of these communities seem to be those where a degree of anonymity has been achieved by the developer and his designer. These houses are so completely without character that owners can, with trees, flowers, window-displays and—if there is a chimney—shows of smoke, improvise a home of their own. The situation becomes more difficult with some loss of this anonymity. One summer, very close to where I live, a group of twenty-five houses was built. After my return from Roumania I passed them every day. One could, at a glance, guess that the developer was in his early fifties, an emigrant from the treeless badlands south of Naples whose sense of paradise had been drawn from the whisky and automobile advertisements in copies of *LIFE* magazine left around by the soldiers of the Second World War. I was absolutely right. There are columns, of course, Parson Capon overhangs, cathedral garage-doors, and artificial window lights and shutters. The houses were not yet occupied but the walls are sparsely studded sheetrock, the floors are plywood and the interiors are clumsy and discordant. No power of exorcism can rid a house of its architect and when the spirit of an avaricious and a stupid man is inexpungeable one finds an appreciable increase in misery, misunderstanding and sometimes crime on the part of the owner. Very early one Sunday morning I drove past this development. It was only a little after dawn and a workman was nailing a vast, green oak branch to the last of the completed roof trees. I stopped and talked with him—shouted at him in fact, since he remained on the roof. "Something has to be right," he shouted back, hammering at the branch. He was doing this on his own time, the idea had come to him in a dream and he was moved by the spirit of an architect, keenly aware of the need for magic in the design of a house where lovers take up their lives and guide the lives of their children and where, without tradition, there is nothing.

We have all found ourselves in Federal Housing Projects or privately owned motel rooms where everything we see, touch, smell and hear urges us to commit murder or suicide or get drunk and perform some contemptible sexual obscenity. The ruins of our great cities—and those spatch-cocked environs whose construction has been motivated entirely by expedience and cupidity represent overwhelming losses of all kinds but they represent to me, much more powerfully than any other work of man, the wages of sin.

John Cheever

ARGUMENTS
IN FAVOR OF SHARPSHOOTING

CHAPTER I
Design in General

Design is the core of all professional training; it is the principal mark that distinguishes the professions from the sciences. Schools of engineering, as well as schools of architecture, business, education, law, and medicine, are all centrally concerned with the process of design.

Herbert A. Simon
The Sciences of the Artificial, 1968

Everything we see in our industrial society is designed and built by other people before we get a chance to use it. Cups, buildings, meadows, and even food are all preceded to some extent by models, drawings or otherwise manifest intentions.

For example, the so-called 'wilderness areas' of the United States exist by design, and quite precise maps of the way they must be kept are on file. The reason for this is partly that a few unspoiled acres will promote greater efficiency by refreshing the work force—or, since very few people actually go there, by providing refreshing images. Even politicians, to the extent that they are social or economic planners, may be considered designers and builders—hence phrases like 'architect of foreign policy'.

All this designing and building is a bit frightening when we consider that other people are making decisions about what kinds of tools, houses, ornaments and even recreation we have available to us. But there are ways in which we can salvage our self-respect as consumers: if we want to, we can repair our own cars, paint our own walls and bake our own bread. And we participate in the design process everytime we buy something, for when we choose a set of dishes or a pair of trousers, we are *not* choosing all the others. In our market oriented economy, consumers still have a way of developing a wariness that will put a designer out of work or a builder out of business if he doesn't do his or her job well enough. It is worth assuming this responsibility since, as Winston Churchill said, "First we design our buildings, then our buildings design us." And it's not just buildings he was talking about—it's everything we buy or pay taxes for that has been designed.

The people who do all this designing are divided into many specialists. The most commonly acknowledged among them are interior designers, product or industrial designers, architects, engineers, urban and regional planners, urban

A house in the Midwest of the United States: the upshot when the desire for a picturesque brick texture meets the trained-in ethos of the Modern Movement.

designers, fashion/textile designers, and graphic designers, These all further subdivide into fascinating sub-specialties. Inigo Jones, The British architect, began as a set-designer in the theatre, for instance. Today he might have been a special-effects technician for the cinema. There are also people who design printed circuits for the electronics industry, which must be assembled under magnification by people of unusual dexterity. There are designers of very specialized medical equipment, such as artificial hearts. There are designers whose works are produced in the billions such as Ray Kroc's masterpiece, the 'Big Mac' hamburger, or Baron Bich's ubiquitous Bic ball-point pen. Sometimes only one item is produced as in *haute couture*, car customizing, space satellite design, or do-it-yourself projects around the house.

Most historians trace the beginnings of 'modern' design to the Bauhaus, a school at Dessau in what is now East Germany. The influence of the approach, teaching methods and philosophy of the school under its first director, Walter Gropius, belies its short life of about ten years before it was closed by Hitler (Hitler believed that the style of Imperial Rome more adequately represented the glories of the Third Reich). Of course, industrialization was underway long before the 1920s, but design was often astonishingly behind the pace of technology during the period before the Bauhaus.

A famous example is that of the handle of the everyday flat-iron. Traditionally this had been made of wood turned on a lathe, but when technology made possible a cheaper, more durable handle of injection-molded Bakelite, the manufacturers continued to produce the same form for many years from molds based on the old handles, so that the shape unnecessarily continued to have more

Moshe Safdie's "Habitat" modular housing project in Montreal. It was built for the World's Fair in 1967. It was a financial failure because of government interference in the economics of the design process, but remains a good example of mass-produced housing.

to do with lathes than with the anatomy of the human hand.

The aim of the Bauhaus was to bring design into step with modern technology. Unfortunately, their enormous progress was often flawed by their desire to create a machine-like *style* rather than to see in the development of new machines and technology better ways of making things fit the hand, as it were. Some of their very elegant and machine-like tea services, for instance, were virtually useless for pouring tea. In dropping design history from their curriculum they may have thrown the baby out with the bath water, for while the period before was ridiculous in its excess of decorative detail there were also traditions of lovely and efficient design quite adaptable for production in an industrial economy. Indeed, the utilitarian beauty of traditional Japanese packaging and American Shaker furniture design is only recently being widely admired again.

The noble intentions of the Bauhaus failed most clearly in the field of architecture, where they achieved their machine-like appearance by carefully covering brickwork with stucco. While it cost a great deal of money in the old days to have intricate decorative carving done, it also costs a great deal of money to have masons lay brick or apply stucco to infinitely greater tolerances than are necessary for structural integrity. Today this trait is so ingrained in the construction industry that it is very hard to get a random pattern or an uneven surface from a skilled worker. This over-precision represents a high hidden cost in our efforts to produce simple, useful buildings.

On the other hand, the design of buildings that not only look machine-made, but actually *are,* is only now becoming feasible. Unfortunately, the construction industry is still largely at the stage of the flat-iron handle; the research and development departments of large materials companies are still hard at work trying to produce a metal shingle that looks just like cedar. Design is catching up, however, and a new wall component is now on the market of foam-injected monocoque steel construction, permanently coloured however you like, that offers the same insulating properties in a two-inch thickness that you would get from several feet of solid brick.

Architecture is always a special problem in design by virtue of the size of its pieces. That is, it is easy to re-tool a manufacturing process to produce a different kind of hand-iron but very difficult to change over a very large component such as a part of a building. Moshe Safdie's famous 'Habitat' housing project in Montreal for the World's Fair of 1967, for instance, turned out to cost twice as much per dwelling unit because the government sponsors cut the size of the project in half. Since the concrete units were poured and steam-cured in an on-site purpose-built factory, a great many units had to be built to achieve what is called 'economies of scale', or in other words, to amortize the cost of building the local factory. Since only half as many units were built as were planned, each unit had to bear twice the amortization cost as it would have otherwise.

DESIGN PROCESS

To understand the design process we have to understand both sides of how an object becomes reality. The process of design is discontinuous by virtue of stages, and normally involves relatively few people—the designers, their clients and consultants. *Design processing* is more immediate and will likely involve large numbers of people—the users.

The first stage of the design process consists of receiving the intentions of the client, whether it is a government, an entrepreneur, a school committee, a family wanting a house, a corporation or whatever. These intentions may be quite specific or quite vague. They may be naive or well-informed. In fact, the clients may not have a specific item in mind at all but only an idea of how it may behave, as in 'something that won't spoil in shipping' or 'something we can sell a lot of'. This is called a performance specification and it is up to the designer to come up with a product that matches the performance of the idea presented to him.

After being presented with the problem, the designer then goes through a process of programming, which consists of both tightening up and amplifying the client's requests. Through her experience in translating needs into objects, and knowing what is possible and what isn't, the designer may even be able to substantively change the client's view of what is actually required. In this phase all the relevant information is gathered, sifted, analyzed and ranked into priorities. Priorities are essential. For example, if two of the client's requirements are to have the design by 1st October, and that the object must be smaller than a breadbox, it does no good to satisfy all the other requirements if the object comes off the drawing board on 5th November and happens to be the size of a car. For complicated projects such as the design of a new town, this programming process may go on for years and involve hundreds of people. The American architect William

Peña has correctly identified the *opportunities* inherent in programming by characterizing it as a problem-*seeking* process.

After the data collecting and programming phase comes the synthesis phase, the very heart of design activity. Here the designer must take all the little bits of information that have been collected—and it may approach millions of bits with the help of computers—and make something out of it that accounts for as many of these bits as possible. Professional design education is crucial here because the mental processes utilized are truly different from the way we've always been taught.

All our schooling up until design education has been linear, atomistic and analytical. That is, we learn to read or to solve problems a piece at a time and in a certain order. Most of our homework is geared to analysis. Writing a school paper is a process of breaking problems, events or issues into their constituent parts and attacking them a piece at a time. Of course when the philosopher Leibniz *discovered* the calculus he discovered it all-at-once—but you can't *teach* it that way. Design synthesis has that all-at-once quality to it, and is most often taught in a studio setting where students solve hundreds of design problems under the direction of studio masters.

The following table is intended to contrast these characteristics of the design process with other kinds of mental processes:

Non-Design Process	*Design Process*
Problem reacting: taking difficulties as they come along.	Problem-seeking: the designer must anticipate problems and hopefully convert them into opportunities.
cookbook: just follow the rules and everything will be fine.	stochastic: this means guessing about results; designers have to be prepared to 'go back to the drawing board.'
serial: one step at a time.	simultaneous-moded: the 'all-at-once-ness' of synthesis.
atomistic-moded: concerned only with detail.	pattern-moded: concerned with several levels at once.
ready-to-wear: selecting.	bespoke: inventing.
non-heuristic: all steps (and results) known in advance.	heuristic: each step has the potential of modifying the next step.

Of course, the characteristics on the right are not exclusively the property of designers as, indeed, not only designers design. Lawyers, physicists, businessmen and poets must be, at different times, adept at many of the things on the right side of the list. Often it is exactly those abilities that distinguish them from their colleagues.

Some people say that you can't teach design at all and that the studio emphasis is on learning by doing. The design process then is a cycle of synthesis-analysis-synthesis, each time trying to positively account for more and more of the bits of programming information, until you decide you're finished or, more likely, run out of time or money. Then the designed item is fabricated, printed, built, cast, grown or otherwise produced. The designer has, or course, taken all the possible methods of production into consideration during the design process and may in fact closely supervise the actual construction.

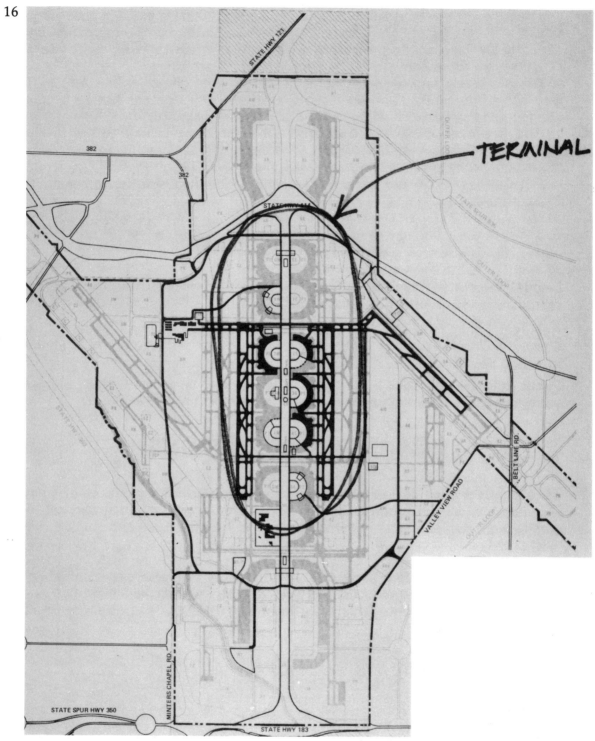

TERMINAL

DALLAS–FORT WORTH AIRPORT

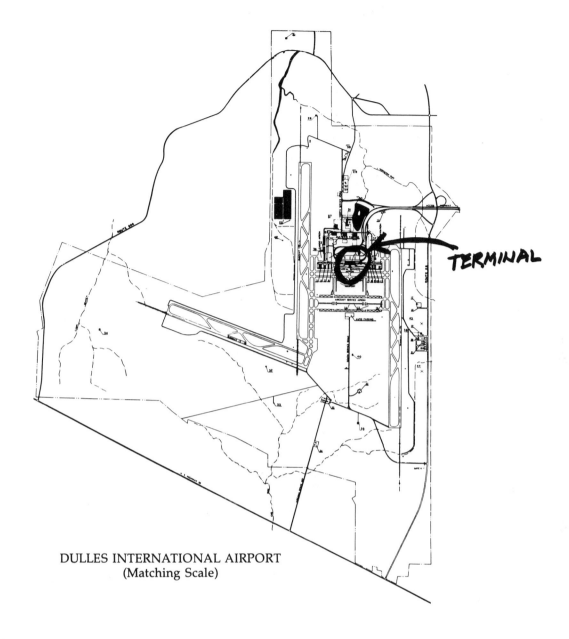

DULLES INTERNATIONAL AIRPORT
(Matching Scale)

CREATIVE DESTRUCTION: THE PARTI SHIFT

Parti is a bit of French slang from the old Ecole des beaux-arts, France's only official free-standing school of architecture from 1816 to 1968. A parti (now a bit of Anglo-American slang as well) is a design concept, sketch or scheme in an early, crude stage of development. It also represents the synthesis we have been talking about. At the Ecole, once a student came up with a parti he was obliged to stick to it and develop it all the way through. Nowadays we realize the enormous value in *not* doing that but instead being quite ready to chuck the whole thing and start over. Instead we view the parti as a hypothesis and if it doesn't pan out for whatever reason we can adjust it or even begin again—but with the difference that we are informed by our failure. This is our cycle of synthesis-analysis-synthesis.

To understand the process a bit better it would help to study two contrasting partis as built: both large, busy airports. An airport is an interesting design problem in that it is as inherently complex as a city yet exists on a much smaller scale. The first is the Dallas-Fort Worth Airport, by architects Hellmuth, Obata & Kassabaum, and it represents the more 'traditional' design yet is the more recently built. The plan is very spikey with long arms and thorn-like branches going off from them. Airplanes are quite large and we want ample maneuvering room between them. We don't want them to touch because their skins are actually quite delicate. This means long distances between different flights of the same airline and very long distances between airlines. Thus one must drive (or be driven) to or from one's airline. For people simply *changing* airlines one might be able to walk but more likely will have to be driven by car, van, cart or some sort of 'people-mover'. So will one's luggage. Since everyone is going in different directions there will have to be a great deal of duplication of shops, toilets, restaurants, etc., as well as transportation to take care of everyone's needs. In any case you now understand the parti: airplanes come directly up to the buildings, drop off or pick up the people inside, and then fly away. Notice that the parti exists (so far) only at the level of a *pattern*. We have no detail as yet. We don't know what planes go where or where the restaurants will be. Neither do we have anything like a precise idea of how many bolts we'll need or where they go. At this point we can apply some very clever and sophisticated mathematical techniques to help us move the pattern-level parti towards a detail-level design. Further, we can use these techniques to insure that the pattern is detailed in the most efficient manner possible—given our *one and only pattern*. We can use our math operations (called algorithms) to minimize or maximize variables (footsteps, gallons of paint, number of restaurants, etc.) while holding other things equal. Indeed, some very special algorithms can even tell us at the *same time* which 'inputs' we could best profit from changing. Again, computers can vastly speed this process up. In fact, if we have more than one parti, or even several, such analysis may help us choose between them.

Now let us consider another, totally different, parti: that of Eero Saarinen's Dulles Airport in the countryside outside Washington, D.C. His parti was that the people would go to the airplanes instead of the other way around. Thus airplanes could land and stop good distances away from the terminal *and* each other, thereby reducing the possibility of catastrophe. Since the terminal doesn't have to stretch out to meet the airplanes, we can have one terminal instead of several and, given the same number of travelers, have a much smaller building area. Also, we can have fewer of everything: bathrooms, shops, restaurants, etc., and still get by very nicely. On a social level, a traveler is as likely to strike up a casual conversation with anyone going everywhere instead of just the same people using his or her airline. When it is time to depart (or arrive) one boards a quiet, comfortable, specially made bus that whisks one to or from one's airplane door to terminal door in three or four minutes. The whole project uses less land and less fuel (buses get much better mileage than jumbo jets at 15 m.p.h.). Here again, algorithms can make the parti more efficient. Indeed, given a range of passengers per day an algorithm can tell you when to use the spikey plan and when to use Saarinen's. Intuitively, it would seem that Saarinen's would be more efficient for very small (skip the buses and walk) and very large, busy airports, with the spikey parti being more efficient at a closed inner range of passenger traffic. These algorithms can, without anything resembling real precision or a "law", nail down that range. What the algorithms *cannot* do is tell you the range of possible partis or invent (design) new ones. Nor can they internally guarantee that the values you've assigned to their variables are correct or that the function truly equals the facility ('eating' doesn't necessarily mean 'restaurant') or that the operational relationships between the variables have been got just right. For science buffs be aware that not only do design syntheses resemble hypotheses but also that parti-shifts resemble scientific revolutions, as described by Thomas Kuhn (*Structure of Scientific Revolutions,* 1962), except that a good designer can do fifty in one day instead of one every fifty years.

EX POST FACTO ANALYSIS AND DEVELOPMENT

Now comes a period of testing known as post-contruction analysis, where the item is somehow measured as accurately as possible to see if it performs as everyone expected it to. For a consumer good this may mean test-marketing to see if anyone will buy it. For a carpet it may mean running an abrasive wheel over it thousands of times to see how it wears. For electrical devices it may mean testing for shock-hazards. For drugs it means long-term testing on animals or volunteer humans. In architecture, unfortunately, this phase is almost never possible, due to the traditional way of budgeting projects and to the enormous complexity of desired or anticipated performance. Most often the architect simply turns to the next project without ever really knowing how the previous one worked out, except for perhaps an aesthetic response from a journalist-critic, often based on photographs rather than a long-term on-site investigation.

Design process is further complicated by the presence of the ego (pride) of the designer. He often suffers from what is called 'the anxiety of influence' (a phrase I owe to Harold Bloom, *The Anxiety of Influence,* 1973) and seeks originality for its own sake rather than for better design. Let's take, for example, the case of the omelette—an ancient and classic recipe for food made from eggs. There is only one way to properly make an omelette and if one follows the rules it is always delicious and satisfying. However, the anxiety of influence drives certain designers (chefs) to modifications, such as adding cheese, bits of bacon, herbs or whatever. These designers are equally looking for a better omelette and for recognition for their brilliant originality, hoping that one day the 'Jones Omelette' or 'Les oeufs à la Jones' will be famous around the world. This seems wasteful, conceited and foolish as long as the original, classic recipe is better or just as good. Except that one day such a chef will bake it instead of frying it, coming up with a quiche or a soufflé—a development that comes to be widely admired and consumed and that cannot be compared to an omelette at all. The designer is often forgotten completely (unfortunately for her ego) and the new product—the soufflé—begins its own period of 'wasteful' and 'egocentric' development, often to cries of 'why don't you leave things the way they are?'

Often, however, self-conscious 'flair' in design leads nowhere, in which case it eventually dies out, much like the tail-fins on American cars in the late 1950s. Unfortunately, such experiments in durable goods such as cars and buildings have to lived with for many years to amortize their cost, as there is too much invested in them to throw them away or tear them down until they wear out. Theoretically, their long-term presence should at least help us not to make the same mistakes again. It's a little early to tell for sure but Place Beaubourg in Paris looks like it might be a candidate for this category.

Related to problems of originality are the issues of 'style' and the underlying tension in the world of design between art and technics. 'Modern' designers, that is designers at least since the Bauhaus, universally imagine themselves to not

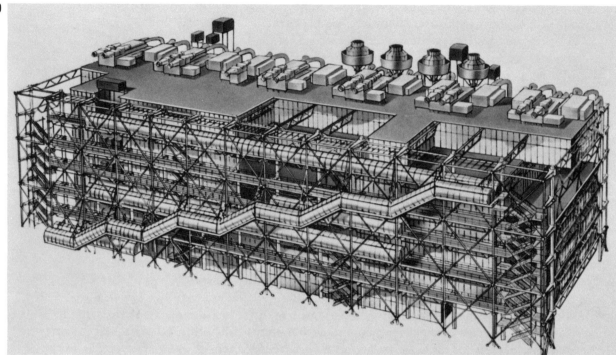

Piano and Rogers' Place Beaubourg, an art palace recently built in Paris. It is the only monument to a radical architectural movement of the 1960s called "Plug-in Architecture" and is likely to remain so. A Frenchman remarked to me, when I asked him what he thought of it, "I will likely come often to the exhibits but I am also glad it is not in my *quartier*."

be working in a particular style. If it was anything at all, the Bauhaus was a reaction against style itself. Yet the Bauhaus style is now instantly recognizable. Throughout history there had been a smooth progression from one style to another: Classic Greek, Roman, Romanesque, Gothic, Renaissance, Baroque, Rococo, and so on. During the Gothic period, for instance, no one would have thought of building any other way. But in the 19th century a knowledge explosion occurred through the widespread use of moveable type and gravure that put all the styles in the hands of any designer who could open a book. This further led to designers travelling around to look at the designs of the past—a professional tradition that continues to this day. Suddenly designers began using whatever style they deemed appropriate: Gothic for churches, Classic for banks, Renaissance for universities, and so forth. Short-lived revivals of certain styles followed higgledy-piggledy as designers became self-conscious about style in a way that would have been unthinkable during the dominance of the individual styles themselves.

The so-called battle of the styles is still partly with us today. While modern designers pretend to abhor such considerations, it is nevertheless true that external observers, professional critics and laymen alike, have no trouble at all classifying designed objects into particular schools of thought. The British architectural critic Charles Jencks is fond of making charts showing the precise placement of contemporary architects according to their philosophical affinities. Of course very few are producing Renaissance design these days, but the Modern Movement has splintered into at least fifteen different recognizable styles as such. One can always tell Swiss packaging graphics when one sees it, as well as Italian furniture design from the late 1960s, or Japanese Metabolist (organic) architecture from the same period.

Some kinds of design are more susceptible to 'style' than others because of their publicness (openness to appreciation) or looseness of program. Design process is always closer to one or another of the two following paradigms. In the 'coin on the table' paradigm the coin is either on the table or off it—there's no in-between. Similarly, a design for a printed circuit or a heart bypass mechanism either works or it doesn't, and no one cares how it looks or what color it is (nevertheless there are examples of both in the design collection of the Museum of Modern Art in New York). In contrast, with the 'sweeping' paradigm one can either do a thorough job, a sloppy job, an artful job (to music?) or a lack-lustre job of sweeping and still claim to have swept the floor in all cases. House design is like that and so is graphic design. In both cases there is room for lots of style, either because the program is so vague or because the basic program is so easily accomplished that the designer feels driven to make more of it than there really is. Thus the tension between art and technics. Are heart-pumps all technics? Are graphics all art? And if houses are to be pursued as art, for whose benefit is it done and at whose expense? New York architect Peter Eisenman designs incredibly complicated and bizarre houses that have their roots equally in the European *De Stijl* (early modern) movement of the 1910s and in images of computer-generated geometric transformations (but laboriously hand-drawn). Yet he has clients willing and even eager to have him design houses where a column literally takes the place of a dinner guest at the table.

One way out of the tension between art and technics for the modern designer has been to approach the design process as if it were nothing more or less than problem-solving. A good example of how this works when it works well is the Vertebra chair, recently designed by Emilio Ambasz and Giancarlo Piretti. The problem was to design an office chair that would be comfortable to sit in for long

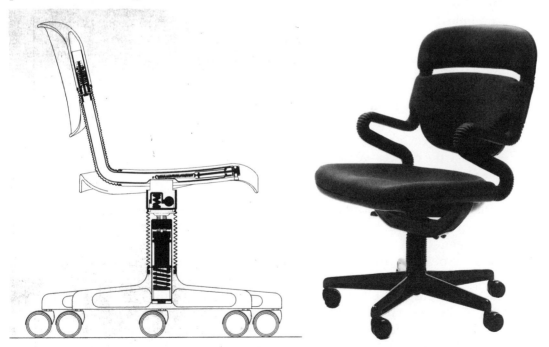

The smartly orthopaedic and genuinely comfortable Vertebra chair, designed by Emilio Ambasz and Giancarlo Piretti. Made and distributed under license from OPEN AfK B.V. (Italy) by Krueger. Technical drawing and photo courtesy of Krueger, Green Bay, WI.

periods of time, and they approached it as a problem, not as an artistic exercise, by making thorough studies of blood circulation, body-shifting cycles and bone structure. The result is a chair that is very comfortable to sit in for long periods of time. There's a bit of style in it too as they have attempted to make it look smartly orthopedic. But it does respond very well to the fact that neither Bob Cratchit's accounting stool, nor the traditional soft and cushy leather club chair, nor the stunning chrome chairs of the Modern Movement were comfortable for any length of time.

There are two problems with the problem-solving approach to design however. One is the suspicion that it is used to somehow 'elevate' the design profession from the mire of art up into a pseudo-scientific stratosphere where the designs are above scrutiny. That it, if it's all no-nonsense problem-solving—and if it seems to solve the problem—then there's nothing to criticize. The other, related, problem is in projects where there might be cultural and emotional content for the users such as in a house. Here, if everything is expressed as a 'problem' there will likely be a good deal of emotional material concomitant with what a house ought to be like that gets passed over simply because these issues do not firm up as 'problems'. Again, it's a responsibility-avoidance situation for the designer and an opportunity for intellectual fraud: designing what you please to satisfy your ego under the guise of solving a limited number of rather obvious problems.

Problem solving may yet be a viable way to ground design but only on two conditions: that the idea of "problem" be expanded to include "opportunity", following William Peña; and that the domain of problems not be limited to empirically defined pin-points but be expansive enough to include the full rich-ness of human action and the textual possibilities of the raw materials at hand to make things with. We have to understand, and harder yet, come to believe, that Louis Sullivan was solving genuine human problems when he was designing his matchless terra cotta ornaments. If you can believe ornament has a function, form can follow it.

The other side of the coin involves *design processing* and instead of involving the designer, now involves the users, consumers or inhabitants. First of all, here's a quote from Robert Sommer, the American psychologist: "Most of us experience the environment just outside of the focus of awareness." What does he mean by that? He means that for the most part we do not use or experience designed objects with the same self-consciousness that they were designed with. We all perform functions through exercising choice but seldom know or care why we make the choices we do. We may think we do not like where we work because the work is dull or the boss is mean when, in fact, we do not like our table or the lighting—and not even be aware of it—or at any rate be able to isolate our dis-satisfactions (or satisfactions, for that matter). We may like a restaurant not for its food or service but because it feels the way we would like our home to be—but can't seem to imagine it really being that way. Yet we think we like going there because of their veal or something else incidental to the mark. In fact, we all stumble about like this, responding much more to advertising and whim than we do to self-conscious efforts to determine how best to enjoy our limited resources.

Studies have conclusively shown that the environment affects us very much, whether we like it or not or whether we know it or not. For instance, if you would like to be chosen foreman of a jury on which you are serving, sitting at either of the chairs marked 'X' (see diagram) will greatly enhance the likelihood of your being chosen by your peers. If the table is round, sit the farthest from the door

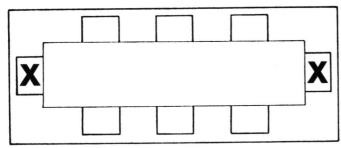

The simulated jury foreman experiment, after the work of Fred Strodtbeck.

to the room. This is an exercise in 'proxemics', or near-space, and has been proven again and again. Some people instinctively sense these things but most of us daily negotiate our environments with some clumsiness. It's very much like the old saying to the effect that we don't know who discovered water but we know it wasn't a fish. The issue in it profoundest sense has been beautifully expressed by the German philosopher Martin Heidegger who said, "Before we build we must first learn how to dwell." Simply put, any effort we make to become more truly conscious of the effect on ourselves of the things or places that we use will be richly rewarded in the increased efficiency of our money, time and capacity for enjoyment.

Several things are at work here in our role as post-product designers (choosers) of the designed object. One is self-expression. If designers can express themselves through the design process, consumers can express themselves through choice as design *processors*. People tend to use objects in a way that best satisfies their need to express themselves. And it turns out, for example, that people who feel the need to design and build their own homes tend to be shy while people who are perfectly happy in furnished hotel rooms tend to be garrulous at the level of clothes and conversation.

The primary way in which our objects serve as vehicles for expression is through association. Associations between yourself and an object can be at any level of human experience: the abstract, the intellectual, the nostalgic, through kinship with nature, dreams, fantasy, *Gemütlichkeit* (coziness) or whatever. Also, stronger associations are built simply by possession. A piece of wood-carving in a museum would mean a great deal more to you if you owned it and even more if you had carved it yourself. And all without any change at all in the object itself. Altering objects increases your associations too, which explains why people bolt on accessories to their cars (or completely rebuild them) or rearrange their furniture (or actually move walls or floors) or do such a simple thing as carve their initials in their school desk. It's as simple as people wanting their things to be like themselves (or how they would like themselves to be), as buffers and anchors in a hostile world, as a way of extending one's domain, as a way of knowing themselves. A cozy, warm sort of man may surround himself with pipes, fireplaces, big soft chairs and a stout old car with some personality to it. A technocratic mobile man-of-the-world would want slick, no-nonsense objects about with lots of buttons to push.

The American industrial designer Jay Doblin has taken the precepts of a school of psychology called transactional analysis and applied its theories to designed objects in a fascinating way. The theory holds that we are each made up of elements of the child, the adult and the parent in different proportions. By looking at a consumer market with a wide variety of choice to it (such as cars) Doblin has picked out three cars as best representing the constituent parts of the personality. They are, in respective order, the Mustang ("for the time of your life"), the Volkswagen Beetle ("a practical car"), and the Cadillac ("for those in command"). When seen in the context of their advertising copy, which strongly reinforces the imagery, it is a very convincing presentation. All three cars can take you shopping. What kind of car do you want to have, and why?

It should be a humbling lesson to designers that their self-expression changes hands at the moment of creation when consumers take over to do precisely the same thing; but then they are already onto expressing themselves through their next design project. As soon as the product is produced, whether it's pantyhose packaging or an office tower, we the consumers could not care less about the designer's ego investment. Their ego-massaging then happens among their peer group of other designers. What we *do* care about is our own ego investment—how well the product reflects what *we* care about—to the extent that we can know. Abstracted to the level of society it is trivially true that those products that are consumed the most mirror exactly that society's priorities. Studies to this point could be termed contemporary archeology—and there are some such studies but probably not enough. However, the process works only to the extent that we are truly aware of the effect on us of our objects and places—and of what they say about us to ourselves and to others.

The other necessary condition for this market to work is that there be a plurality of like-function objects for consumers to discriminate between. This again raises a special problem in the field of architecture. While we have an enormous variety of bars of soap to choose from—and even cars, due to economies of scale—we do not have that much choice regarding architecture, for several reasons. One is that the professional community is relatively small and therefore incestuous. While there are only 489 people for every doctor and 430 people for each lawyer there are 3333 people for each architect (U.S.A.). This is rather a small cadre to whom to entrust the design of much our visible, public, physical environment. Also, there are professional filters, such as standard national exams, curricula and professional societies that give awards always to the same sort of buildings. No wonder much of it comes out looking alike.

It is an interesting note, now that we are entering the era of 'post-modern' design, as some (Joseph Hudnut first; *Architecture and the Spirit of Man,* 1949) call it, that several writers are speculating on the possibility that for the last forty years no one except the architects themselves and a very few like-minded critics have liked modern architecture at all. This raises the question, essentially an ethical one, regarding the apparently monolithic behaviour of the architecture profession: is it a good thing to keep trying for the quiche or the soufflé if the process in the meantime makes the omelette unavilable?

In short, there is less choice for the consumer user in the field of architecture to enable her to express herself. In the special area of single-family housing (in which architects seldom participate in the U.S.A.) builders use the same design over and over again because (1) a new design means slower progress by a work crew dealing with the unfamiliar and (2) most builders are small operators with a lot riding on each unit, which naturally tends to conservatism in design. So the market, within a given price range, has less of the variety found in soaps and cars. This reason, plus the price of new construction, is what drives young people on both sides of the Atlantic towards older houses, even if they are in need of substantial repair. There are more opportunities for self-expression in the range of older houses available.

In non-residential building architects do not deal with the users directly, but with clients, who are more and more a faceless group of accountants, businessmen, lawyers and bankers. Clients who do not want to hear one dissenting voice from among their stockholders tend to insist on faceless buildings, like television producers who do not want to offend sponsors. Increasingly restrictive bureaucratically generated codes, standards and regulations also contribute, and so do problems in the work force. If you want to design a picturesque building, as we mentioned earlier, you will have a hard time finding a mason who can lay brick or apply stucco in an irregular manner and you likely cannot find a stone- or wood-carver at all. And if you want to design a very modern building with cost-saving unitized prefabricated bathrooms you will have to pay four plumbers to stand and watch the crane operators put it in place. These sorts of difficulties are not encountered by the graphic designer or even the appliance designer. They are quite free to innovate and often do. Furniture and appliance design are in fact miles ahead of architecture for these very reasons.

The last item to mention is something common to some extent to all professions. This is the concept of 'poets in the profession', a phrase I owe to U.S.C.'s Robert Harris (in conversation). These are people in each field of design accounted as the 'architects' architect' or the 'engineers' engineer'. Oddly enough, these people are seldom the best of their peers in the strictly professional sense of the word. Their car designs may not allow enough room for luggage, their fashion designs may be terribly impractical as protection from the elements, their buildings may leak, their bridges may be dishearteningly fragile, their graphics may never cover a famous magazine. Often these people have trouble finding enough work to keep busy and are notoriously bad businessmen. But they serve an important function by reminding the rest of the profession that it also has in it the power to lift the human spirit.

In our brief look at the nature of design—a background necessary to the case investigation which follows—we have seen that designers are fellow (meaning that there are many more similarities than differences with non-designers) men and women who have developed, one way or another, some special (but certainly not unique) mental capacities. Under the most severe reduction these boil down to the ability to do all-at-once synthesis well.

In the chapter which follows we will narrow the field of design to architecture and limn the case by tracing the long development of a single epidemic problem in architectural design: succumbing to the temptation to reduce the amount and variety of data one has to synthesize. For the competent designer such a reduction makes the work easier; for the poor designer it may make it possible. In the medium term, as we have now, the society that desires otherwise loses. In the long run architecture's short-cuts contain the seeds of its own doom, since at some point society will simply quit paying for an inferior product. This has already commenced.

To trace this development will require vast prolegomena. "Architecture" will not even be mentioned for two score pages. I beg your patience by invoking W. H. Auden ("Letter to Lord Byron," Collected Poems, 1976):

> *"It's possible a little dose of history*
> *May help us in unravelling this mystery,"*

CHAPTER II
The Rise of Empiricism in Architecture

"The state departments of several nations are today using games theory, backed up by computers, as a way of deciding international policy. They identify first what seem to be the rules of the game of international interaction; they then consider the distribution of strength, weapons, strategic points, grievances, etc., over the geography and the identified nations. They then ask the computers to compute what should be our next move to minimize the chances of our losing the game. The computer then cranks and heaves and gives an answer, and there is some tempta-tion to obey the computer. After all, if you follow the computer you are a little less responsible than if you made up your own mind. But if you do what the computer advises, you assert by that move that you support the rules of the game which you fed into the computer. You have affirmed the rules of that game. No doubt nations of the other side also have computers and are playing similar games, and are affirming the rules of the game that they are feeding to their computers. The result is a system in which the rules of international interaction become more and more rigid."

Gregory Batson
Steps Towards an Ecology of the Mind, 1972

PART ONE: To World War II

In The First Volume of Either/Or *Kierkegaard describes a romantic nihilist. His aesthete no longer tries to draw away the veil hiding the infinite; he does not believe in a saving beyond in even this weak and rather foggy sense. He finds himself alone and bored in a world which is indifferent to his demand for meaning. Yet the demand for meaning persists. Despairing of discovering meaning, he attempts to invent it and thus to escape from the absurdity of his situation.*

Karsten Harries
The Meaning of Modern Art, 1968

A NEW PHILOSOPHY

Times were not very happy in the period before World War I. Germany had been unified by "blood and iron" and embarked late, but aggressively, into colonial expansion. Austria annexed Bosnia in 1908, and the Balkan Wars of 1912-13 made everyone uneasy about the rising tide of nationalism and expansion. The

Viennese financial crisis of 1873 precipitated a panic in New York as well, marking the beginning of tied international economic crises, increasingly industrial in nature rather than just financial. The 1907 panic was severe enough to cause the creation of the U.S. Federal Reserve System.

Times were not very happy during the war. The U.S. stayed out until the last year, missing three-fourths of the bloodshed. The 'Great' War saw the first tanks, submarines, camouflage, automatic pistols, flame-throwers, airplanes, poison gas and numbers on the order of ten million dead and twenty million wounded. War was no longer burnished boots and the smell of the campfire.

Times were not very happy after the war. Lord Keyne's *Economic Consequences of the Peace* (1919) documents how Wilson offered gracious terms to coax the Germans into surrendering early and then sandbagged them with embittering reparations and humiliating conditions. Starvation and epidemics took hundreds of thousands more. There was no Marshall Plan. Demogogues and inflation rose almost immediately and within ten years there was a depression that lasted ten years.

Ex-nihilism, but clearly not *ex-nihilo,* there arose like "lilacs out of the dead land," apposite philosophies. Nietzsche's *Übermensch,* now that he was safely dead, began to be twisted into notions of national and racial superiority; never mind Nietzsche's life-long contempt for state governments, particularly German ones. Kierkegaard, unknown outside of Denmark during the 19th century, along with Karl Jaspers and many others later, offered Existentialism, whose key tenent is that existence precedes essence, rather than the other way around, meaning that if you want any meaning in your life, you must create it on your own. The corpus of existentialism remains largely unread but it has affected millions through its vague diffusion in novels and films.

The movement that concerns us, however, is the victorious one. It was founded by a group called the *Wiener Kreis,* or Vienna Circle, and was rung around a man named Moritz Schlick, who studied physics under Max Planck at the University of Berlin until 1904 and accepted (as the first scientist to do so) the chair in philosophy at the University of Vienna in 1921, the same year Wittgenstein's *Tractatus Logico-philosophicus* was published. Wittgenstein, an engineer turned philosopher, had studied under Russell at Cambridge during the period that Russell and Whitehead were writing the *Principia Mathematica,* a work of mathematical logic that Russell was later to claim permitted one to say nothing either wrong or important. While not a true member of the *Wiener Kreis,* Wittgenstein remained both close and important to the group as did the physicist and mathematician, Karl Popper.

The issue was that philosophy should be more, in fact, exactly, like science. The key criterion was that anything that could not be empirically verified was neither true nor false but only meaningless. Thus, as with the existentialists, there was no 'hope'. Nor could one discuss the dark side of the moon (before the satellite went around it). Metaphysics were impossible and ethics and values were problematical. Schlick was shot and killed by a crazed graduate student in 1936 and the Vienna Circle broke up. It has never been taught in German-speaking countries (but there was a meeting group in Berlin) and has indeed been outlawed in Eastern European countries, which is ironic as it has been routinely been accused of 'collectivist' tendencies and one of its founders, Otto Neurath, was an outspoken Marxist. The name of the movement is Logical Positivism.

Adherents most often draw their lineage to Auguste Comte (d. 1857), a French philosopher who sought to reconcile science with religion and to develop, on a scientific basis, what we later came to call sociology. He regarded science as the third "positive" stage (after theology and metaphysics) of evolution, wrote the six-volume *Cours de Philosophie Positive,* and tried on several fronts to unify all the sciences. At the same time, looking far into the future, he foresaw, but did not decry, a "despotism based on science." Closer in time is the work of Ernst Mach (d. 1916), a physicist who despised metaphysics and was to later have a profound effect on Percy W. Bridgman, author of the 1927 *Logic of Modern Physics,* a bold attempt to cleanse science of all "operationally undefinable terms" which in turn ought to have made unifying all the sciences easier. Thus, in time, they not only wanted to make philosophy, sociology, psychology, economics, etc., more like science, they also wanted to make science more like Logical Positivism.

Wiener Kreis members Hans Hahn (a mathematician), Otto Neurath (a sociologist), and Philip Frank (a physicist) had already begun meeting in 1907. When physicist Schlick came in 1921 at their urging, the Circle enlarged to include engineer Kurt Gödel (or Goedel), mathematician Rudolph Carnap, historian Victor Kraft, lawyer Felix Kaufmann, economist Karl Menger, Béla von Jukos (or Juhos) and students Friedrich Waismann, Ludwig Von Bertalanffy and Herbert Feigl. Frequent foreign visitors included the Finnish psychologist E. Kaila, Berlin philosophy student Carl Hempel and Oxford philosopher A. J. Ayer. By 1928 they were calling themselves *Verein Ernst Mach* (the Ernst Mach Society). When Schlick returned from a year at Stanford in 1928, his followers greeted him with a manifesto called *Wissenschaftliche Weltauffassung: Der Wiener Kreis* ("The Scientific World View: The Vienna Circle").

There were several good reasons why Logical Positivism flourished when it did. First of all, science was in a phase of "creative destruction": in a few short years science was shaken to the core as the Euclidean-Newtonian Universe turned into vapor. X-rays, radioactivity and the electron all showed that the atom was not what it was thought to be. Einstein's Special Theory of Relativity of 1905 dissolved physics and mathematics in a world still debating Darwin's theories of evolution and Mendel's work in genetics. Indeed, explaining Einstein's work to the world took most of Schlick's energies from 1910 to 1920. Heisenberg added uncertainty to relativity when he showed that attempting to "see" an electron meant moving it with a quantum of light. Secondly, it appeared that crass technology, perpetrated by amateur inventors, was out-stripping science. Currently emerging technology such as refinements in electronics, computers, and fiber optics are mere candle points compared to the explosion between 1875-1905. Virtually everything we take for granted today appeared in that period: cellophane (1869); duplex telegraphy (1872); street lights and telephones (1876); phonographs (1877); shift-key typewriters (1878); shipping frozen food, electric railroads and power plants (1880); AC-DC transformers (1881); alloy steels and turbines (1882); motion pictures (1885); elevators (1887); followed by skyscrapers (1890's); electric automobiles and incandescent lamp manufacture (1891); radios (1895); airplanes and automobile mass production (1903); rayon, teletype and vacuum tubes (1904); Diesel engines and plastics (1905), etc. While inventors were quickly gratified (if their inventions worked and were patentable), scientific advances were quite slowly vindicated. On the other hand, scientists formed societies, inventors did not.

But most importantly, the world was no longer readily understandable and the events of mankind—social, political, economic, and technological—seemed out of control. The local atmosphere has been brilliantly described by William M. Johnston in his *Vienna, Vienna* of 1980:

> "The two and a half decades from 1890 to 1914 saw Vienna at the height of her creativity. During those years Viennese writers, artists, and thinkers pioneered attitudes that would spread throughout Europe and North America after 1945. Many of the most far-seeing thinkers were fascinated by a sense of decline, of deliquescence, of insecurity. They assumed that things would not go on as they were for very much longer... The Viennese *fin de siècle* has become for us a fascinating outburst of prophecy and insight before the First World War spread disillusionment and desperation to everyone."

And elsewhere:

> "At a time when it was forbidden to debate matters of fundamental principle, scholars retreated into collecting data. We have the paradox that censorship promoted scientific positivism in the sense that attention was focused on establishing collections of data rather than discussing their significance. The practice of collecting by private citizens reinforced the bias toward positivism that already haunted the bureaucracy. To place themselves above reproach, Metternich's civil service cultivated an ideal of objectivity about matters that the twentieth century recognizes as laden with value judgments."

Richard Neutra, living in Vienna in 1920, writes his friend R.M. Schindler in Los Angeles, "Perhaps (you think) Europe is ahead of the U.S. in its tradition, in a finer and more developed class structure, practical estimation, conservation, treatment of all cultural values, a more spiritual, less hectic life which was the result of a certain affluence. All of this disappeared, is discredited, refuted." (from Dione Neutra's unpublished *Promise and Fulfillment*).

The existentialists saw world war, starvation, and the breakdown of old orders and declared that man had no inherent meaning. The great advantage of abiding by the Positivists' verification principle was that it vastly reduced the number of questions. The circumscribed world that remained was their secure repository of meaning in a world being spun by invisible hands. By attempting a unified philosophy of science, they sought to build a foundation under it in the same manner that St. Thomas Aquinas, through Aristotle (translated from Arabic to Greek to Latin), built a foundation for Christianity. In confused, menacing times, people prefer easy answers even if (and perhaps even more so if) very complicated processes generate them.

Yet there is no graspable connection between a desire to purify science and a desire to extend (or equivocate) scientific procedure into what were hitherto not considered areas of scientific inquiry, such as economics, history, psychology and sociology. Here Logical Positivism became teleological (purposeful) and, indeed, messianic. In 1930 the *Wiener Kreis* took over a journal and renamed it *Erkenntis*, changed in 1938 to the *Journal of Unified Science*. Carnap and Hans Reichenbach were the editors through 1939 when publication halted. It resumed in 1975 with Carl Hempel as the U.S.A. editor. Hempel was at Princeton, where Gödel had gone, and had studied in Vienna and Berlin under positivist teachers. During those years an international following began: the American C. W. Morris built the bridge to Charles Pierce's Pragmatism and Czech-born American Ernest Nagel visited Carnap in Vienna, having studied logic under Whitehead at Harvard. Nagel wrote a very influential American article, "The Fight for Clarity: Logical Positivism" for the *American Scholar* in 1938. The Russian-born American philosopher Max Black wrote *Theories of Logical Positivism* in 1939 but never published it. He had studied math at Cambridge with Jacob Bronowski, both of whom were influenced by their teachers, Russell and Wittgenstein. Oxford philosophers Gilbert Ryle and A. J. Ayer attended positivist meetings in Vienna and Ayer later edited a book titled *Logical Positivism* (1959). Their mentor, G. E. Moore, gave the opening address at the Positivist Congress in 1938. Bertrand Russell and, to some extent, A. North Whitehead, had been more or less adopted by the Positivists because of their work in mathematical logic. Hans Hahn was an expert on the *Principia*, the theory of logical types, the division of elementary (atomic and molecular) and generalized statements, and the principle of abstraction, all of which were quite useful concepts to positivist logicians. Schools cropped up in Scandinavia and Poland as well, while Germany remained largely aloof.

The move into other areas had already begun. Carnap pronounced ethics meaningless and psychology a branch of physics. Indeed, Carnap and Neurath declared the language of physics appropriate for all branches of knowledge. Sociologists, psychologists, economists, etc., for whom this had appeal, joined the movement and began adapting appropriate methodologies for their own fields. There is no doubt of their seriousness in this regard. Hempel spent years later searching for the scientific laws of how *history* unfolded.

As the Nazis rose to power in Austria, the Vienna Circle dispersed. Many of the members were Jewish and anti-Semitism had raised its awful head. Neurath went to the Hague in 1936 and started the Institute for the Unity of Science, later moving it briefly to Boston. Frank went to Harvard. Feigl went to Minnesota. Gödel went to Princeton. Hahn died in 1934 and Schlick in 1936. Felix Kaufmann also went to the U.S. Popper went to the London School of Economics and Waismann went to Oxford. Wittgenstein went to Cambridge in 1929 and Carnap went to the University of Chicago which, in 1938, agreed to publish incrementally the *International Encyclopedia of Unified Science*. As of 1962 Otto Neurath, as always the movement's head publicist, was the Editor-in-Chief with Rudolf Carnap and Charles Morris as Associate Editors. Two volumes had been published as of that date with chapter titles such as *Linguistic Aspects of Science, Principles of the Theory of Probability, Cosmology, Foundations of Biology, The Conceptual Framework of Psychology, Foundations of the Social Sciences,* and *Methodology of Mathematical Economics* and *Econometrics*. The series also included the influential *Structure of Scientific Revolutions* by Thomas Kuhn. Chicago was also hospitable to one of the best known positivist (which architects call Rationalist) architects, Mies van der Rohe, who in 1938 became the Chairman of Architecture at the Illinois Institute of Technology and was charged with redesigning their entire campus, which he did. By 1960 we have Arthur Drexler's (*Ludwig Mies van der Rohe*) assessment in his second paragraph: "He made art seem rational, as if it were science."

Karl Jaspers, the existentialist, said in 1913 (*Allgemeine Psychiatrie*) that the positivist approach to psychotherapy was hopelessly deterministic. The German phenomenologist, Edmund Husserl, father of that school of philosophy and active shortly after 1900, argued that empiricism was abstracted from reality and that when phenomena were forced through man-made systems they became quite different phenomena. Empiricism was a reduction of truth and empirical statements were probable at best. Yet the work of American physicist, Willard Gibbs, (d. 1903), so well articulated by Norbert Wiener in *The Human Use of Human Beings* (1950) satisfies your author in passing between the horns of phenomenology and scientific empiricism by introducing a thorough-going application of probability theory into physics. There may or may not be laws but if there are they are abstract. Measurement is also not abstract but it is also never exact. Probability provides the methodology to come close, however, and even to estimate how close, thus enabling one's predications to be about measurements rather than laws. 'Laws' can, indeed, be induced to a high state of dependability through constant conjunction over great lengths of time but cannot be really "posited." But the Logical Positivists were, with some irony, *hoping* for laws, not truth as normative science knows it, and the fewer and more comprehensive the better. Oddly enough, some of the greatest lasting contributions of the mathematicians connected to the movement, namely by Carnap, Nagel and the Pole Tarski have been precisely in the area of probability and mathematical logic.

Economist Ludwig von Mises in *Human Action* (1949), criticized the movement in this way:

"Outside of the field of economic history nobody ever ventured to maintain that constant relations prevail in human history. It is a fact that in the armed conflicts fought in the past between Europeans and backward peoples of other races, one European soldier was usually a match for several native fighters. But nobody was ever foolish enough to 'measure' the magnitude of European superiority.

The impractibility of measurement is not due to the lack of technical methods for the establishment of measure. It is due to the absence of constant relations. If it were only caused by technical insufficiency, at least an approximate estimation would be possible in some cases. But the main fact is that there are no constant relations. Economics is not, as ignorant positivists repeat again and again, backward because it is not "quantitative." It is not quantitative and does not measure because there are no constants. Statistical figures referring to economic events are historical data. They tell us what happened in a nonrepeatable historical case. Physical events can be interpreted on the ground of our knowledge concerning constant relations established by experiments. Historical events are not open to such an interpretation."

And on describing methodology notes the following:

"The various schemes proposed can be classified in the following way:
1. Calculation in kind is to be substituted for calculation in terms of money. This method is worthless. One cannot add or subtract numbers of different kinds (heterogeneous quantities).*"

Footnoted:
"*It would hardly be worth while even to mention this suggestion if it were not the solution that emanated from the very busy and obtrusive circle of the 'logical positivists' who flagrantly advertise their program of the

'unified science.' Cf. the writings of the late chief organizer of this group, Otto Neurath, who in 1919 acted as the head of the socialization bureau of the short-lived Soviet republic of Munich."

Economist F. A. von Hayek gave English currency to the word "scientism" (meaning science where it does not belong) but claims he borrowed it from the French, who have been deviled by positivism ever since Comte. Von Hayek comments in *The Counter-Revolution of Science* (1955):

"Their (the physical scientists) science was such that they came to exert an extraordinary fascination on those working in other worlds, who rapidly began to imitate their teaching and vocabulary... These latter became increasingly concerned to vindicate their equal status by showing that their methods were the same as those of their more brilliantly successful sisters rather than by adapting their methods more and more to their particular problems."

Richard M. Weaver, writing in *Scientism and Values* (1960) says:

"The founders of scientist sociology did not so much arrive independently at a definition of sociology (in doing which they would have been scientists) as seek identification, for external reasons, with another field of study. In proceeding thus, they were not trying to state the nature of their subject; they were trying to get a value imputed to it."

And finally, Albert Camus, in the 1942 *Myth of Sisyphus*:

"Hence the intelligence, too, tells me in its way that this world is absurd. Its contrary, blind reason, may well claim that all is clear; I was waiting for proof and longing for it to be right. But despite so many pretentious centuries and over the heads of so many eloquent and persuasive men, I know that is false ... That universal reason, practical or ethical, that determinism, those categories that explain everything are enough to make a decent man laugh. They have nothing to do with the mind. They negate its profound truth, which is to be enchained. In this intelligible and limited universe, man's fate henceforth assumes its meaning ... In his recovered and now studied lucidity, the feeling of the absurd becomes clear and definite. I said that the world is absurd, but I was too hasty. This world in itself is not reasonable, that is all that can be said. But what is absurd is the confrontation of this irrational and the wild longing for clarity whose call echoes in the human heart."

TOWARDS WW II

While Logical Positivism as a specific movement died out in the late thirties, world empiricism had been moved as if by a lever through the movement's efforts. First culture gives rise to an apposite philosophy and then the philosophy returns to influence the culture. For one thing, the invasion of mathematical science into new areas began to have new, genuinely useful applications. To find the roots that were to express themselves in another discipline, engineering, requires us to return to the *Umwelt* of French empiricism from which Logical Positivism itself sprang.

Systems analysis had pre-*Wiener Kreis* origins as far back as 1794, the date of the founding of l'Ecole polytechnique. The Revolution had swept away the system of colleges and universities and friend of Napoleon and father of descriptive geometry, G. Monge, along with his former pupil the revolutionist and physicist Lazare Carnot, suggested the founding of l'Ecole, which from its inception overshadowed its predecessor, L'Ecole des ponts et chaussés (bridges and roads). L'EPC was job specific; l'EP trained engineers to do whatever needed doing. As the charge to engineers broadened its educational base narrowed. Severely diminished in the new curriculum were the beloved literature, grammar, history, languages and moral instruction. The new Rationalist/Enlightment enthusiasm saw the founding of such societies as l'Association Philotechnique (*sic*) and the Sociètè Polytechnique. Balzac noted the peculiar characteristics of the new "type" as those who "prided themselves on having more precise and satisfactory solutions than anyone else for all political, religious and social questions." It was in this atmosphere that Saint-Simon conceived his fantastic plans for reorganizing society and where the positivist Auguste Comte and hundreds of Saint-Simonians received their education. Saint-Simon, protean positivist and socialist remarked (*Oeuvres de Saint-Simon et d'Enfantin*, 1865-1878): "It is necessary that the physiologists chase from their company the philosophers, moralists and metaphysicians just as the astronomers have chased out the astrologers and the chemists have chased out the alchemists." Born to wealth, Saint-Simon lost all his money in foolish business ventures and in his poorer days was taken in by his former valet, only to be rescued in the summer of 1817 when the young engineer/philosopher Auguste Comte joined him for the last eight years of Saint-Simon's life. Comte is now regarded as the founder of sociology. Napoleon III declared himself a Saint-Simonist, much as Nixon declared himself a Keynesian. From this point on engineering and science began their slow, inexorable convergence. Engineering was subsequently well-represented in the *Wiener Kreis* by Mssrs. Gödel, Wittgenstein and Richard (not Ludwig) V. Mises.

Whether Logical Positivism was a boost rather than a first cause is incidental to the fact that a revolution took place in engineering over the years from being task specific (military machines, fortifications, bridges, canals, etc.) to being process specific. Engineering became a professional cluster of algorithms (dedicated processes leading to closely-nested goals). As the quiver of algorithms increased, first arithmetically, and then geometrically, engineers were increasingly led to believe that they could do anything. Engineering had become 'holistic'.

By the outbreak of hostilities systems analysis and systems engineering were already in place in American industry. In management Mssrs. Frederick Taylor and Henry Gantt were trying to "systematically" analyze labor to optimize that resource as a factor of production. By the thirties Norbert Wiener, who had also studied mathematics at Cambridge before starting to teach at MIT, was working with Vannevar Bush on computers to solve problems in differential equations with more than one variable and with Yuk Wing Su on electrical network design at Bell Telephone Laboratories. Around them was a growing welter, on both sides of the Atlantic, out of which was born systems analysis (and its subset cybernetics) and operations research.

Consider the problem of constructing a building. An endless amount of time could be devoted to gathering factual information about this situation: for example, the precise location and physical characteristics of the building; a detailed study of the climatic conditions of the potential sites and the influence these will have on construction costs; the sources of the funds used and their cost. Most importantly, the decision maker might decide that he must consider specifically and in detail all potential uses of the funds in this period and in future periods. If our decision maker adopts a strategy of collecting all *the facts before he acts, it follows that he will never act. The human mind cannot consider every aspect of an empirical problem. Some attributes of the problem must be ignored if a decision is to be made.*

Mssrs Bierman, Bonini & Hausman
Quantitative Analysis for Business Decisions, 1977

OPERATIONS RESEARCH

The sea-change that science and mathematics had undergone since 1890 was that while the *phenomena* of the world were unchanged our *view* of it was no longer deterministic and static but was now probabilistic and dynamic. As Jacob Bronowski says in "The New Scientific Thought and Its Impact," in Volume VI, Part One of the 1966 UNESCO *History of Mankind:*

"In extensions of traditional mathematics there was evolved a new basic concept: the concept of the operation. It caused mathematics to be regarded not as a set of numbers held together by equations but as a set of structures turned into one another by operations . . . The mathematician came to see himself actively as a man who carries out new operations."

It does not *necessarily* follow, as the construct of the world became less certain, that science would become any less rigorous. But it certainly could become more supple and it could, and would, seek out areas of human action for investigation that its previous character made less tempting than it now was.

Just as Frederick Taylor is cited by the systems analysts as their civilian antecedent, so is Horace Levinson cited by the operations research people. An astronomer, Levinson went to work for the L. Bamberger department stores in the twenties and applied a 'scientific' approach to merchandizing. His work for them was still an industrial secret thirty years later.

The birth of military O.R. is generally accorded to have occurred with the formation of Blackett's Circus and, especially, its removal in May of 1936 to the coastal Bawdsey Research Station to work on radar strategies. A physicist, Patrick M. S. Blackett had organized the group, which consisted of such people as Solly Zuckerman, the Capetown anatomist; physicist Jacob Bronowski (later); engineer W. N. Thomas; biochemist R. B. Fisher; geneticist C. H. Waddington; physicist J. D. Bernal; F. A. Lindemann; L. M. Denbitz and I. N. Pincus. By the summer of 1940 they had signed, several of them, a manifesto to the effect that many factors regarding the War could be reduced to numerical values and thus optimized (or minimized). On the U.S.A. side, physicist Philip Morse and chemist George Kimball are credited with getting military O.R. development into print first. Morse was educated at Case and Princeton and taught at MIT. Later he was to become a Trustee of RAND and the first president of the U.S. Operations Research Society (1952). Such distinguished scientists as Norbert Wiener worked on ballistic problems in a way that was to become known as cybernetics. U.S. military O.R. was less concentrated and more wide-spread than in England and many people had in fact started doing it without knowing it, much as the Molière character spoke prose. Actually, our first overt plunge had been taken by Wiener's colleague, Vannevar Bush, the great MIT engineer, who visited Bawdsey Station and reported to the Air Force on the techniques were in place there as of that date. By V-J Day there were 26 O.R. groups active in the Air Force. Morse and Kimball had been simultaneously working for the Navy.

In any case, history documents several stunning successes directly due to the efforts of these Allied groups:

1) Depth charges—some quite simple calculations regarding U-boat dimensions, attack approach speeds, dive speeds, etc. resulted in a change in the depth at which the charges would explode. Kill rates increased from 400% to 700%, depending on whom you read.

2) Some calculations on radar deployment by Blackett's Circus vastly increased Britain's early warning system.

3) Calculations on historical data regarding convoy losses led the U.S. to increase convoy size for a great overall reduction in losses. A similar effect was had by increasing the size of bombing raids.

4) Studies of sweep rates and day versus night attacks greatly reduced German security in the Bay of Biscay.

5) Gaming theory applications in the Sea of Japan permitted the U.S. Navy to out-guess the Japanese again and again.

6) Calculations showed that under Kamikaze attacks large ships should maneuver violently and small ships turn slowly.

By the end of the War there was little question of the utility of operations research and the infrastructure began to fill in, first in the military. The OAG (Operations Analysis Group) performed for the Air Force, the OEG (Operations Evaluation Group) performed for the Navy, and the ORO (Operations Research Office) performed for the Army. The ORO was contracted out to Johns Hopkins, which quickly laid in a supply of Case Western alumni and began work on Army O.R. problems. One of the more interesting problems, which came in short order, was to ascertain whether or not to give economic aid to Europe. Paralleling these inhouse capabilities, quangos (quasi-governmental organizations) and private consulting groups with such names and abbreviations as Aerospace, ANSER, Arthur D. Little (which Kimball joined), HUMMRO, RAC, RAND, SDC, SORO, and SRI sprang up like mushrooms. RAND was founded in 1946 when the Air Force gave Donald Douglas of McDonnell Douglas $10 million to do so. Two years later it moved to the West Coast with Ford Foundation support. RAND (an acronym for 'R & D') became one of the best known and Bruce Smith (*The RAND Corporation,* 1966) says "The character of the work performed by the principle defense advisory organs usually has centered around operations research." He also notes that while O.R. was started by mathematicians and scientists it soon came to be equally well-represented by economists and sociologists. He also reminds us that President Eisenhower, in his farewell address of January, 1961, warned us not only of the "military-industrial complex" but also that ". . . public policy could itself become captive of a scientific-technological elite."

Meanwhile positivist Rudolf Carnap was supplying RAND with a steady flow of graduates: Herbert Simon, Olaf Helmer (the originator of the Delphi technique), H. Bohnert, Norman Dalkey, Abraham Kaplan, Albert Wohlstetter,

Sidney Davidson, and many others. Eventually RAND was to have as many private clients as public and to house as many industrial secrets as national security secrets. Such private sector developments distinguished American growth from England's. The English groups continued to flourish in the Civil Service but in the U.S. O.R. quickly spread to the emerging consultative industry and the schools; first at Case Western (C. West Churchman, R.L. Ackoff); then at MIT (Wiener, Morse, William Higgins); Johns Hopkins (the U.K.-born Ralph Gibson, the Israel-born, Case PhD Eliezar Naddor; Richard Zimmerman and Charles Flagle); and Michigan (Anatol Rapoport, the Russian-born games expert who had studied under Carnap). An interesting development is that while England's stuffy *Wissenschaft* university system resisted O.R., the Commonwealth's did not and O.R. took hold with a vengeance in less culturally secure outposts such as Australia, New Zealand and South Africa. Associations began to form as well, with the separate but similarly named Operations Research Societies opening their doors in both the U.S. and U.K. in England, the latter hosting a 21 nation congress in 1957.

The differences and similarities between O.R. and systems analysis began to be (and still are) debated. In general, O.R. consists of a nested set of algorithms whose common element is the application of probability. Some of these are:

1) Expected value—if I have a 20% chance of winning $1 I have an expected value of 20¢.

2) Decision Theory—"decision trees" built up by expected values of discrete actions. Strategies of minimizing maximums and vice versa.

3) Game theory—this was first developed in the Sea of Japan maneuvers and was vastly enlarged by the milestone publication of the *Theory of Games and Economic Behavior* (1944) by John von Neumann (a Hungarian-born chemical engineer who had served in the O.R. group of the Naval Ordnance Laboratory during the War and as "Johann von Neumann" gave a paper at the 1930 Positivist Congress at Konigsberg) and Oskar Morganstern (an economist). At Princeton with Gödel and Hempel, German-born Morganstern had both studied and taught at the University of Vienna from 1925 to 1938. When Mssrs. Morse and Kimball sat down to write *Methods of Operations Research* (1950) they had already been strongly influenced by the work of von Neuman and Morganstern and said so.

4) Linear Programming—the 'Simplex Method' was developed by George Danzig for the Navy during the War. This algorithm is an iterative process, comfortably at home in computer software, that determines the sensitivity of various inputs to output and has powerful applications in distribution, manufacturing and deployment—if the assumptions are correct. It is also closely related to game theory. Danzig later went to RAND, and then to Stanford, where he applied his theories to city design. These latter experiments resulted in tower concentrations that sound remarkably like Le Corbusier's *Ville Radieuse.*

5) Queuing theory—a related set of operations that has found numerous domestic applications for which we can be daily thankful: one-way tolls on bridges and single queues to always free tellers in bank lobbies. Such seemingly common-sensical changes have saved millions of person-hours and dollars since their innovation.

6) Simulation—while all of the above involved simulation (indeed, Bronowski has called mathematics not factual but the most colossal metaphor of all time) simulation can properly be called a class of operations by itself. Architectural models (and even drawings) are simulations. Anytime one reduces

reality to make it easier to deal with, manipulate or operate on one is using simulation.

Rudolf Penner, Director of the CBO (Congressional Budget Office) has the entire U.S. economy 'modeled' or simulated in his computers. David Stockman, President Reagan's director of OMB (office of Management and Budget) has his own similar set of econometric equations. Paul Volker, Chairman of the Federal Reserve Board, has yet a third set. The fact that the three produce wildly different results is not encouraging. The fact that when the predicted point in time arrives and events prove to correlate only randomly to the predictions of all three is even less encouraging. The man who (currently) is widely believed, and thus whose pronouncements make the stock market go up and down, is Salomon Brothers' Henry Kaufman, who just sits and thinks—and whose power rests on his being correct more often, indeed, far more often, than any of the econometric think-tanks.

SYSTEMS ANALYSIS

For systems analysis there is no such set or taxonomy of operations to define the field. It is more properly a process, and a much more general one than any of the above. Ralph E. Gibson outlines the process's characteristics in his 1960 article "The Recognition of Systems Engineering" in *Operations Research and Systems Engineering* (edited Charles Flagle, et. al.). Gibson lists six and for each compares them to the system of the human body:

1) Well-defined functions—in other words, clear intentions as to how the system will perform.

2) Feedback control—this is the kernel of cybernetics. The system has to be self-regulating.

3) Protection of the critical function—for the human system this is to reason.

4) Ultrastability—this means that the feedback loop has close, critical limits. Human body temperature oscillates very closely around 98.6 degrees F.

5) Redundancy—Meaning ample excess capacity. We can lose ¾ of our kidney, ⅓ of our brain, ½ of our lungs, etc. and still function.

6) Reliability—the system must work dependably.

It is generally agreed that operations research was born of scientists and mathematicians while systems analysis was born of engineers. At the 1958 Conference on Education for Operations Research at Cornell, Dr. Alex Boldyreff remarked that in general O.R. involved changes to the extant (changes in procedure) while systems engineering was the design of the new and usually involved changes in equipment. He also remarked that the results of the latter were more often more "verifiable" than those of the former. As examples of O.R. that typify these characteristics he cites the mining of the Sea of Japan strategy, the large convoy strategy and the integration of the Negro into the armed forces. As examples of systems engineering he gives the design of the proximity fuse, the telephone system, and the guided missile.

Systems analysis, with the added dimension of *Gestalt* psychology, becomes something else called systems theory and its base shifts from engineering to a more general scientific community. *Gestalt* psychology comes to us largely from Wolfgang Köhler (1887-1967), an Estonian-born psychologist who also studied physics under Max Plank. Indeed, there had been a small empiricist "Berlin group" active at the same time as the *Wiener Kreis*. It was called the *Gesellschaft für empirische philosophie*. Among its members were cross-overs Hans Reichenbach and Carl Hempel as well as Alex Herzberg, Walter Dubislav, Kurt Lewin and Wolfgang Köhler. Köhler came to the U.S. in 1935 and taught at Swarthmore and Dartmouth. *Gestalt* psychologists insist that the whole of anything is greater than the sum of its parts and, indeed, has its own intrinsic laws and behavior, which they sought, and still seek, to discover.

The chief promulgator and author of systems theory was Ludwig von Bertalanffy (d. 1972) who studied under Moritz Schlick in Vienna and taught there until 1948, when he immigrated to Canada, settling down in 1962 at the University of Alberta.

In 1954, at the Stanford Center for Advanced Study in Behavioral Sciences, Bertalanffy, economist Kenneth Boulding, games theorist Anatol Rapoport and biologist Ralph Gerard formed the Society for General Systems Research, later to become an affiliate of AAAS. The best sources for information about the movement are the society's yearbooks, *General Systems,* and Bertalanffy's own writings. By Bertalanffy's account, systems theory was a thankless mission he pursued as a lonely hero until three great ideas came together closely in time: Norbert Wiener's *Cybernetics* (1948), von Neumann and Morgenstern's *Theory of Games and Economic Behavior* (1944) and *The Mathematical Theory of Communication* (1949) by Claude Shannon and Warren Weaver. He then lists a taxonomy of his field subsuming the above as well as simulation and other theories under the rubrics of classical, set, graph, net, game, decision and queuing, etc. His purview, as detailed in his 1948 *General System Theory,* ranges from biology to psychology to urban problems, education and the military-industrial complex. A successor, James Miller, has produced a very large and colorful text called *Living Systems* (1978) that begins with a cell and continues through an eyeball, a body, a group, an ocean liner, an organization, society, the Netherlands and supernational organizations as more or less analogous open systems.

The last general off-shoot, and one that parallels all the others from the very beginning, is linguistics. Isolating the utility of either systems theory or semantical analysis (or semiotics, etc.) is not easy; for the most part they are pursued, from your author's point of view, as philosophy, or, as its practitioners would likely prefer it, pure science. None-the-less, its utility may simply not be easily trackable as yet. Of the three principals of Mead Data Central (before a recent purge by parent Mead Corporation) one was a physicist who specialized in systems, one was a Ph.D. in political science, and one was a semanticist-linguist, who charmingly referred to the consequences of imbibing too much at dinner as "post-prandial narcolepsy." It is quite clear that as computer technology shifts increasingly to language applications, voice commands, and searches of echoing data bases from numerical operations that such approaches to language will be of more and greater utility.

All of the early positivists were centrally concerned with language. Russell, Whitehead, the entire *Wiener Kreis,* including and, indeed, especially Wittgenstein and Popper, all had language as a central concern, either in its informal mode or as symbolic logic. As engineer Richard (not Ludwig) von Mises remarks in *Positivism* (1956):

> "1. The first, still unconscious, step in the urge for sciences, i.e., for intellectual comprehension of the world, is the creation of language.
> 2. Grammatical rules in the widest sense of the word are conventions which, corresponding to a more primitive stage of intellectual development, establish certain simple typical relations and force us to reduce, in some manner, everything that we want to express in words to these basic relations.
> 3. Progress in scientific knowledge is possible only if it is accompanied by a critical and conscious attempt at the improvement of language. The gradual creation of a comprehensive 'language of science' is a part of this improvement."

By August of 1943 the Society for General Semantics had published the first issue of *Etc.: A Review of General Semantics* under the editorship of S. I. Hayakawa, now a retired U.S. Senator. Deeply involved from the beginning was the ubiquitous games theory expert Anatol Rapoport from the University of Michigan's Mental Health Research Institute.

APOSTASY AND REDEDICATION

Finally apostasy begins to appear. Bertalanffy rejects Logical Positivism in "The Psychopathology of Scientism" in *Scientism and Values,* 1960, and elsewhere. Bronowski, in the October 1951 issue of *Scientific American* doubts that operations research has a post-War future and that in any case it is "hardly likely to be rewarding to first rate scientists." Norbert Wiener, taught by Hahn and Russell, followed suit in publicly rejecting systems analysis. Like all apostasies, however, there is an element of simple swerving from precursors in each case.

Since Logical Positivism was firmly identified with the Vienna Circle—and that was now a dead horse—it didn't hurt to flog it a bit if you thought you might have a better chance of unifying science with your own much livelier steed. At the same time Wiener was apostatizing he was proclaiming cybernetics as the herald of the Second Industrial Revolution. At the same time Bertalanffy was apostatizing he was claiming cybernetics (a word Wiener invented) was a small subset of systems theory and that general systems theory was the best hope we had for unifying science since everything was part of one open system or other. He elaborates in *General System Theory* (1968):

> "We believe that the future elaboration of system theory will prove to be a major step towards unification of science. It may be destined in the science of the future, to play a role similar to that of Aristotelian logic in the science of antiquity. The Greek conception of the world was static . . . Therefore classification was the central problem in science . . . In modern science, dynamic interaction appears to be the central problem in all fields of reality. Its general principles are to be defined by system theory."

As well, in his introduction to *General System Theory* Bertalanffy quotes from Russell Ackoff's "Games, Decisions and Organizations," published in the *General*

"In the last two decades we have witnessed the emergence of the system as a key concept in scientific research. Systems, of course, have been studied for centuries, but something new has been added.... The tendency to study systems as an entity rather than as a conglomeration of parts is consistent with the tendency in contemporary science no longer to isolate phenomena in narrowly confined contexts, but rather to open interactions for examination and to examine larger and larger slices of nature. Under the banner of systems research (and its many synonyms) we have also witnessed a convergence of many more specialized contemporary scientific developments.... These research pursuits and many others are being interwoven into a cooperative research effort involving an ever-widening spectrum of scientific and engineering disciplines. We are participating in what is probably the most comprehensive effort to attain a synthesis of scientific knowledge yet made."

Ackoff was an architecture graduate from Penn who did his Ph.D. at Lancaster, finally coming to roost at Wharton as the dean of American operations researchers concerned with management. In the next *Yearbook* (1960) he published "Systems, Organizations, and Interdisciplinary Research", in which he defended the founding of the Systems Research Center (there were several of like ilk already) at Case by saying:

"I believe the systems movement will reach fruition in an interdiscipline of wider scope and greater significance than has yet been attained ... I consider operations research as an intermediate step toward this fruition ... I believe systems engineering and operations research are rapidly converging."

Karl Popper was apostatizing as early as 1934 in *The Logic of Scientific Discovery*. Of the lot, the ones with the best motives in doing so seem to be Popper and Bronowski. The former because he was, in the long view, happy with science the way it classically was (and is); namely that no one cares where hypotheses come from—the important thing is providing good faith efforts to prove them wrong. He even attaches a letter from Einstein (including facsimile) agreeing with him. Einstein, by-the-by, incapable of an unkind word, had nothing to do with the movement his entire life. He thought the verifiability criterion silly and believed that hypotheses were simply "invented." Turning the telescope around, it was invention that Bronowski cared about most. His apostasy, like C. P. Snow's anxieties over the "two cultures," was mired in defending imagination. The last refuge of the humanist (especially converts) is to protect the imagination against science (as if it needed it).

In any case, the apostasies are about, generally, those tenets of Logical Positivism which are, from a cultural point of view, trivial. The positivists denied the Neo-Platonic speculations that led to Kepler's Laws and held that Democritus had no business postulating atoms. Now they take it back. And since we now have famous astronomers who have never peered through a telescope and physicists who will never see their particles when they discover them we had best forget about direct empirical verification. However, if certain of the tools to unify science were to prove foolish the goal lives on and flourishes behind the apostasies of its professors and their successors.

In its new forms empiricism has penetrated every discipline that was penetrable. Linguistics and geography were unrecognizeably transformed. Even the deep core of the humanities was not left untouched. Berlin-born Rudolf

Arnheim was brought to the New School for Social Research by his teacher Wolfgang Köhler. Arnheim reassures us in the Introduction of his *Toward a Psychology of Art,* 1966, that:

> "A pyramid of science is under construction. The ambition of the builders is eventually to "cover" all things, mental and physical human and natural, animate and inanimate, by a few rules. The pyramid will look sharp enough at the peak, but toward the base it will vanish inevitably in a fog of stimulating ignorance like one of those mountains that dissolve in the emptiness of untouched silk in Chinese brush paintings. For as the base broadens to encompass an ever greater refinement of species, those few sturdy rules will intertwine in endless complexity and form patterns so intricate as to appear untouchable by reason. The prospect is challenging but also frightening. In particular, we may feel tempted to approach the individuality of human nature, human actions, and human creations in an attitude of defeatist awe. To reject all generalization in this field looks good. Who would not like to be the one who respects the ultimate mystery of all things? With the smile of the sage one can, without effort, watch the sacrilegious and clumsy manipulation of the professors. It is an attitude that triumphs in conversation and noncommittal criticism. Unfortunately it gets us nowhere. Psychology as a humanistic science is beginning to emerge from an uneasy rapprochement between the philosophical and poetical interpretations of the mind on the one hand and the experimental investigations of muscle, nerve, and gland on the other."

Such an expression is powerfully teleological and, for those who know Lovejoy's *Great Chain of Being,* astonishingly medieval in its cultural longing.

Finally, however, Bronowski went much further with his 1965 supplement to the new edition of *The Identity of Man*—a last chapter called "The Logic of the Mind." He draws our attention to Gödel's Theorem of 1931, the first part of which asserts that any 'rich' system of logic can express true assertions that can't be deduced from its axioms. The second part says that axioms can't be shown in advance to be free of hidden contradictions. This is the same Gödel from the *Wiener Kreis.* Bronowski continues:

> "Such a system of axioms has always been thought to be the ideal model for which all science strives. Indeed, it could be said that theoretical science is the attempt to uncover an ultimate and comprehensive set of axioms (including mathematical rules) from which all the phenomena of the world could be shown to follow by deductive steps. But the results that I have quoted, and specifically the theorems of Gödel and of Tarski, make it evident that this ideal is hopeless...
>
> I hold, therefore, that the logical theorems reach decisively into the systemization of empirical science. It follows in my view that the unwritten aim that the physical sciences have set themselves since Isaac Newton's time cannot be attained. The Laws of nature cannot be formulated as an axiomatic, deductive, formal and unambiguous system which is also complete. And if at any stage in scientific discovery the laws of nature did seem to make a complete system, then we should have to conclude that we had not got them right... There is no perfect description conceivable, even in the abstract, in the form of an axiomatic and deductive system."

And thus one road to unity comes to a dead end for those who believe Bronowski's interpretation of Gödel; but since the teens in Vienna there has been a steady extension down another road in case the search for the set of laws failed. Perhaps, in retrospect, it was the best strategy after all, for if we cannot unify science as discrete from everything else, it follows that science would be *de facto* unified if there *were* nothing else. Thus, by 1950, Anatol Rapoport's *Science and the Goals of*

Man is published, and S. I. Hayakawa's Foreword is not timid about its intentions, worth quoting at length.

"Dr. Rapoport's basic concern in *Science and the Goals of Man* is that of many other students of general semantics as well as of many other philosophers of science. Is science 'merely a tool', or can it be a way of life? According to a belief widely held among scientists no less than among humanists and men of letters, science does not, should not, and ultimately cannot determine the ends for which it is used. This view, entailing a sharp separation of science and values, Dr. Rapoport regards as a tragic fallacy. The fallacy rests, as he demonstrates, upon an imperfect insight on the part of scientists themselves into the ethical implications of their own scientific behavior.

Scientists, no less than others, instead of observing their own behavior and its implications, tend to believe what they say about themselves. Because they have been, up to now, deeply preoccupied with throwing off the prejudices of local limited value-systems in order to clarify their vision, they have hesitated to impose their own value-system on others; they have usually talked (and many still talk) as if their scientific patterns of evaluation had no validity or application beyond the fields of their scientific activity.

Nevertheless, the scientists 'prejudice' against prejudice—that is, their preference of a general and nonpartisan point of view over a point of view colored by private or provincial obsessions—is a value necessary in all areas of life. The same is true of other value-preferences exhibited in the behavior of scientists: the preference of truth-telling over lying, which is so much a part of scientific tradition that no machinery is needed (as it is in almost all other human affairs) to enforce honesty; a preference of statements capable of verification over statements that must be taken on the authority of the speaker; a preference of logical order over the chaotic assemblage of facts.

All these preferences, Dr. Rapoport affirms, may be organized into a value-system capable of being subscribed to by all men—a value-system of which the most general directive is the preference of human agreement (and therefore co-operation) over disagreement. Like the logical positivists, Dr. Rapoport is impatient with nonsense questions and unverifiable statements, not simply because they are nonsense, but more importantly because they are among the greatest obstacles to human agreement. Confronted with a variety of competing ideologies and value-systems, the scientist, *in order to be consistent with himself,* cannot remain neutral. As Dr. Rapoport says, different men want to go in different directions, and some of these directions are incompatible with the direction inherent in science itself. Therefore, the scientist must subscribe to certain values (and discard others) not because he is a 'good citizen' or a product of a [particular] culture or a member of a [particular] church, *but because he is a scientist.*"

We have come a long way since the members of the *Wiener Kreis* declared ethics meaningless.

PART THREE: Science, Technology, Education and Society

We look for experiments that shall afford light rather than profit, imitating the Divine Creation, which, as we have often observed, only produced light on the first day, and assigned that whole day to its creation, without adding any material work.

Francis Bacon
Novum Organum, 1620

TO THE VICTORS GO THE SPOILS

Directly behind the allied forces' entry into Germany, and sometimes ahead of them, were teams that dearly wanted to evaluate Nazi progress in science. Despite rumours that the Nazis were close to developing a nuclear weapon, it was clear upon arrival that they were in fact years away from it. A chief handicap was that anyone with any brains had left in the thirties, as we have seen. In addition, there was considerable political meddling in scientific affairs which hampered work. Finally, the Nazis believed wrongly (on both counts) that the War would be short and that 'science' necessarily takes a long time. In any case, allied scientists were perfectly willing to take credit for winning the War, having developed a taste for federal funding while doing so.

The fact that the War had been won by technology and not by pure science is a point scientists largely do not care to dwell upon. The equivocation between the two is a gavotte pure science manages very well. The pure research underlying the atomic bomb was published before World War I by Einstein, although key advances in technology lay years in the future. Yet the National Academy of Sciences was, and is, perfectly happy to simultaneously deny membership to Dr. Jonas Salk (because the 'pure' research had been done years earlier that led to the Salk polio vaccine) while taking full credit for winning the War. Finally, the official science establishment has time and again behaviorally rejected Bridgman's concept of operationalism by defining science according to *who* does it, not by *what* is done. The War effort was very 'applied', very technological, very engineering oriented, as we have seen. But to the extent that scientists were involved it was all deemed scientific work. Technologists and engineers were and are willing to put up with this flogging, much like John the Scot was willing to put up with the drunken abuse of King Charles the Bold, not because they ate better in so doing but because they got above the salt. A symbiosis began to develop where the scientists lent their prestige in exchange for productivity and the engineers traded autonomy for proximity. The capacity for such manipulation has been colorfully described in three somewhat quixotic characteristics by Daniel S. Greenberg in *The Politics of Pure Science,* 1967:

> "... the inhabitants of the scientific community are, first of all, reverently patriotic toward the methodology and mores of their craft. Secondly, they are anxiously poised to expel intruders who would usurp the name of science or meddle in its internal affairs; and finally, they simply wish the rest of us would convert to science. Let us say that this trinity of characteristics can best be summed up as chauvinism, xenophobia, and evangelism ..."

Both the National Academy of Sciences and the American Association for the Advancement of Science are middle-nineteenth century organizations. Along with architecture, science was one of the few avocations a nineteenth century gentleman could pursue and still remain a gentleman. Both the NAS and the AAAS, however, founded organizational sections for engineering in the teens which have since received just enough spiritual sustenance to never leave the nest. As recently as the Hoover administration, federal expenditures (total) for applied research were $200 million while only $10 million for pure. Scientists can be remarkably pragmatic about dowries.

In 1945 MIT engineer Vannaver Bush, who had played masterful roles during the War in orchestrating the science war effort and pacifically walking the line between applied and pure research, wrote Truman proposing a scientific foundation—one that would be isolated from political influence (unlike the entire rest of the government). In other words, an unfettered pipeline to the Treasury. Aside from the scientists' victory laurels, the government was disposed to help out of fear of depression—a fear that we forget pervaded American society in the immediate Post-War era. The universities simply couldn't hire the scientists who had gone to war unless their research was sponsored by someone—and the government did not want them out of work. The Congressional debate over the nascent foundation was hot and furious, with Senator Harley Kilgore insisting for five years on combining basic and developmental research—but the scientists would have none of it. But when they indeed got their way in 1950 they were funding operations research and systems analysis projects, as science, within eighteen months—the Office of Engineering *Sciences* (author's emphasis) having opened in 1951. The National Science Foundation dabbled in technology, often outside their Congressional mandate, from the beginning. They need the fruit of technology to display at appropriations time. They also need technology because it's a font of science. But they also wanted, and got, founding legislation that left no doubt as to how pure and applied science ranked in their "great chain of being". The first Director of the National Science Foundation was Alan T. Waterman, who had to resign his position as director of the Office of Naval Research to accept his new post. The first year's funding was for $225,000. By the end of the year of the Sputnik, 1957, Eisenhower had his very own full-time science advisor (a first). In 1966 funding was $207,000,000, a largess only exceeded by the *other* $293,000,000 pure science funding received directly from the Department of Defense. By 1968 NSF had secured Congressional amendments to permit it to pursue 'applied' research and by the mid-seventies it had funded a University of California/Berkeley architecture professor's salary for a year to have him conduct a study on whether the NSF should open an architecture section. NSF appropriations in FY 1982 broke the billion dollar mark ($1,000,000,000) for the first time—but remember that is a *fraction* of the Fed's total R & D outlays. More than any other free nation the U.S. funds its research through the unlikely Medici of national defense.

SCIENCE ≠ TECHNOLOGY

Despairing of all other attempts, and likely without a thought of Bridgman in his head, Yale's Derek deSolla Price ("Toward a Model of Science Indicators" in *Toward a Metric of Science,* 1978) offers us the following definitions:

"The outputs of technology are economically valuable goods and services;

the outputs of science are publications into the world system of scientific information."

Is science a consumption good yielding direct utility, such as poetry or fine painting, or is it an investment good, meaning an input to production? On a clear, warm, optimistic day scientists prefer the former. Duke's Philip Handler, past Chairman of the National Sciences Board and the President's Science Advisory Board, on one of those days, remarked that "the edifice which is being created by sciences ... is fully comparable to the cathedrals of the Middle Ages ..."

When testifying for appropriations, however, they prefer the latter. While it is hard to demonstrate that they are rather worse than tendentious on such occasions, it is even harder to prove the contrary. Again from Greenberg,

> "It is not improbable that the French monarchy saw intrinsic validity in the theory of the divine right of kings. When the statesmen of pure science proclaim that pure science is the locomotive of contemporary society, their sincerity is equaled only by their lack of evidence."

Historically, technology has been the provider of new opportunities for scientific study. The steam engine gave rise to thermodynamics, not the other way around. The inventors gave us the Industrial Revolution; the scientists published. British universities had nothing whatsoever to do with the Industrial Revolution. Another source of science is Pasteur-like problems that arise in industry, which are solved or not solved, and end up either way in scientific journals. Yet another source is instrumentation. True, Einstein sat in a Swiss civil service office and turned physics upside-down in three papers, but most scientists today are lost without instruments—some of which come at dozens or several scores of millions of dollars each, such as linear accelerators. The paradigm is not nearly so much Popper's falsification of hypotheses as it is the appearance of the technical instrument. Galileo's telescope was a by-product of a flourishing spectacle lens grinding trade. In the same category are the thermometer, barometer, electrostatic generator, vacuum pump, etc. The influence of instruments (in its broadest sense, to include such things as censuses) obscures the tenuous relationship between science and technology because it actually (but inobtrusively) powers both of them. DeSolla Price writes, in his unpublished 1982 NSF Report "The Science/Technology Relationship, The Craft of Experimental Science, and Policy for the Improvement of High Technology Innovation.":

> "Thus the dominant pattern of science/technology interaction turns out to be that both the scientific and the technological innovation may proceed from the same adventitious invention of a new instrumentality. In science the typical result of such a major change is a breakthrough or shift of paradigm, in technology one has a significant innovation and the possibility of products that were not around to be sold last year. There is therefore a correlation of sorts between the scientific and technological events and it is this, without doubt, that is the basis of the common but misleading presumption that somehow the scientific advance has produced the technological 'application'."

Again following deSolla Price, innovation has more to do with market pull than with technological availability. Most innovation that actually comes to pass does so because it is demanded in the market place. Also, most of it, indeed, virtually all of it, are extensions of an extant body of knowledge. Leonardo da Vinci did the 'basic' research on the helicopter in 1500. It was not sufficiently demanded between 1500 and 1900. If the Milanese had been taxed $100,000 to give Leonardo a grant to research such a device then they would have had to wait 400 years for its fruition. Assuming a modest average discount rate of 5%, the opportunity cost of their taxed-away money would have amounted, by the time it was delivered, to 2.9×10^{13} (meaning shift the decimal point 13 places to the right). On a per capita basis the most expensive research being done today is in particle physics. Excluding medicine it is the most expensive, period. In November of 1983 the Department of Energy decided to abandon the $200 million sunk cost in the Brookhaven National Lab's atom smasher in favor of a more powerful $2 *billion* accelerator. Total federal outlays for physics research in FY 1982 (basic and applied) were $1,396,255,000. That is the sum of the annual tuition, at my nearby junior college, for 2,792,500 youths. It also represents 28,000 modest houses. What they are after is one more elusive, ephemeral particle, called a "W Intermediate Vector Boson," leading towards "GUTS" (Grand Unified Theories). The reason they want to find it is to unify science (you can start at either end).

No one questions that solving the morphology of the atom is interesting. Or that the result will not be beautiful. What one questions is when it will provide jobs for southern Illinois. And if the answer is never, or in a very long time, then we can better use the money for something that might help those in need now, or at least sooner. But suppose what the scientists specially plead to Congress were true? Suppose the fruits of their labor did quickly lead straight to productive, job producing technology? If it did, neither southern Illinoisans, nor any Americans, would be uniquely benefited for the expenditure of *their* tax dollars *because basic research is an internationally free commodity. Basic research is openly published, not patented.* Even if science were a direct consumption good, even if it were like cathedral building, the analogy still would not hold. The cathedrals, after ten centuries, are still in France, not in Japan. The omelette and souvenir shops at Mont St. Michel are earning revenue today exactly as they did in the year 1000. In the long run (and spectacularly so in the short) it made much more sense to build cathedrals than it would have to give da Vinci a grant. There are now close to 50,000 scientific journals being regularly published.

HIGHER EDUCATION AND WORK STYLES: PUZZLE SAWYERS AND PROBLEM SOLVERS

During the nineteenth century, and for the first half of the twentieth, higher education in England, the U.S., and Continental Europe developed along different paths. When Continental statesmen turned to higher education for the trained minds deemed necessary to emulate the British Industrial Revolution, science and the pure pursuit of knowledge so dominated the classical university that despite the long establishment of law, medicine and theology, the other professions were unable to gain university acceptance. The problem was resolved when national leaders, such as Napoleon, Bismarck, and the Kaiser lent their prestige and authority to the founding, separate from the traditional university, of the Technische Hochschulen for the professions. The early success of the Hochschulen, as well as Napoleon's Polytechniques, led to a three-way separation into *Kunst* (art), *Wissenschaft* (the scientific approach to all formally expressed knowledge), and *Technik* (the useful). Today, *Technik* is generally taught in Europe in separate technical universities quite apart from the classical universities that teach *Wissenschaft. Kunst,* the fine arts, is taught in a number of separate schools and conservatories.

Across the English Channel, higher education did not divide. When Parliament belatedly realized Britain needed, but did not possess, a version of the Technische Hochschule, the leaders of educational thought in Britain were under the spell of Cardinal Newman's (d. 1890) lectures, Mark Pattison's (d. 1884) essays, and the classicist Benjamin Jowett's (d. 1893) teaching. It is not surprising, therefore, that they opposed the segregation of technological education into separate institutions. Thus the traditional English University provides education in the arts, sciences, and professions. But the *sequential* establishment in English higher education of liberal learning, followed by the sciences and *finally* the professions, left a British bias toward the arts and science. This viewpoint is most clearly expressed in C. P. Snow's "Two Cultures." Snow sought to improve man's lot by seeking a bridge between the two cultures of the arts/humanities and the sciences, with no consideration or recognition that national wealth is largely created by the third culture of the interposed professions. The British desire to ignore Technik results in some amusing habits, such as calling engineers 'scientists', and the creation of bureaus for 'science policy', which tend to exclude the professions. It has had some not so amusing results as the professional schools aped the sciences to gain academic respectability while ignoring the pressing needs of the country. Michael Fores, in an article entitled "Applied Science is Pure Nonsense in Myopic Britain," *(London Times,* 19 March 1979) summarizes the syndrome by observing:

> "... it is the foundation of the slow suicide of a group: a sure way of how not to succeed as a nation without really trying to discover why. Any grasp of the *Technik* concept would help in this discovery."

Meanwhile, in the U.S., the great state universities created through the Land Grant system by the Morrill Act of 1862 emphasized agriculture and mechanics. The state universities were technical-professional schools turning out the basic practitioners of engineering, teaching, manufacturing, management, architecture and (especially) agriculture that were needed to build a nation. That these "aggie" *Techniks* were wildly successful through the 1950s is a matter of historical record.

Unfortunately, the prestige and financial power of the NSF, together with a government supported public fascination with science, has severely warped the fabric of U.S. higher education by stimulating the growth of classical universities at the expense of land grant institutions and rewarding those land grant institutions which substantially shifted from *Technik* to *Wissenschaft.* Even departments legally excluded from NSF's chartered mandate managed to either secure grants under the rubric of science or responded through emulation to the peer pressure of their colleagues' research and teaching styles. As well, just as other colleges on campus became more like science, so did other federal granting agencies became more like the NSF.

At the time when U.S. technology and professional management were being recognized throughout the world, a counter-trend was beginning to develop in the U.S. universities. The visible signs of achievement and national recognition afforded by a NSF grant became irresistible on the campus. The warming flow of prestige, graduate students and promotions that accompanied the flood of science money found no natural enemy to maintain the normal balance in the academic jungle. One hundred years of Land Grant tradition was slowly but steadily replaced by the basic research orientation of the English and pre-WW I classical German universities. However, without the balancing existence of institutions like the continental Polytechnique or Hochschule, we are now repeating English history in demonstrating that possession of scientific knowledge does not easily translate into economic strength or improved life quality.

The case of the School of Criminology at the University of California at Berkeley is a classic case of things gone wrong. In this example, the school was formed when the state realized that while a large percentage of its resources were expended for the state's police departments, there was not a single first-rate institution for professional education in criminology in the West. Recognition for the school came rapidly as professional contact and cooperation were established with law enforcement agencies. Within roughly a decade, the school established the guidelines and standards for modern police work throughout the state. Then, responding to academic criticism that its professional work was outstanding but that it had not done quite enough basic research, the school sought and appointed a few research sociologists. Easily meeting the new university criteria for promotion and tenure supported by federal granting agencies, the sociologists prospered and bred more of themselves. These professors, however, were not sympathetic to the practical professional problems of the police. With time, the split became so great that members of the School of Criminology, who were very busy with their research anyway, were no longer welcomed by the police departments and the professional contact died. Ultimately, in its regular review of its schools and colleges, the University examined the faculty and found it to be staffed with sociologists who were undertaking research that the University concluded could be conducted just as effectively in the Sociology Department. This question of redundancy must ultimately be faced by every professional school that forsakes *Technik* for *Wissenschaft* against its charter and public trust. Down the coast, at U.S.C.'s Music School, Jascha Heifetz was denied tenure because he hadn't published enough.

Neither the American public (nor your author) are opposed to education in, and the free pursuit of, basic research at public expense. Nor does the author strictly relegate basic research expenditures to the consumption side of the educational spending equation while claiming that all applied, professional and vocational expenditures constitute the true vial of the investment side. What is true is that the *balance* between our great public and private universities (*Wissenschaft*) and our equally great Land Grant colleges and universities (*Technik*) has been destroyed and when the public and the students are getting the former when they paid for the latter we have in fact, as a society, crossed the line between investment and consumption.

Specifically, the rise of research gave rise to the research degree, the Ph.D. It is also called the "terminal" degree, meaning not only that there is no further degree but also that it is preceded in an orderly fashion by a bachelor's and a master's degree. The traditional model for professional schools, however, has been the "first professional" degree, meaning that degree which permits one to sit for licensing exams or to be directly licensed. Once one has that degree it makes no sense for one to have an 'advanced' degree in the same subject. Indeed, an *Architectural Record* study of 1967 showed that while holders of the M. Architecture degree had somewhat higher salaries for their first five years of employment than their colleagues with B. Architecture degrees, there was no difference thereafter. Thus, one would suspect, and one finds, a great deal of lateral movement in professional education. An engineering student may well find a MBA useful and an architecture student may find a MCP useful. In fact, both have been formulae in the past. One is expected to hone one's skills (however many are acquired) in practice. Further, opportunities for lateral movement in disparate degrees are vast. An MCS (master of computer science) is rising in popularity. Carnegie-Mellon offers an excellent Masters in Construction Management that attracts architects, CE's and business majors alike. Doctors can choose from dozens of specialties for further study.

There is an isomorphism between such academic progress and the way professionals actually work (see illustration). Professionals are always generalists in the sense that their work charges a lattice, with the fruits of the last move influencing the vector of the next. The task of all professionals is the general one of allocating resources. Within their chosen field they are constantly ranging the extent of it because of the inherently stochastic nature of the problems they are asked to solve. Further, Derek deSolla Price (*"The Science/Technology Relationship—"*, op. cit.) uses cocitation analysis to describe the progress of science thusly:

> Each [scientific] paper in turn shows its locality by the place in the map and the company it keeps within its invisible college sub-specialty domain, and each paper shows its strength or weakness by the extent to which it causes the map to deform and grow faster at its particular location [see illustration]. The entire design has some similarity to crystal growth, or to the piece-by-piece solution of some giant jigsaw puzzle proceeding outward from a central core laid down at the beginning of the cumulation in the mid-seventeenth century invention of the scientific paper (if not before). Each annual cocitation map is laid down like successive skins of an irregular onion. Cut a section through the onion and it looks like a jigsaw puzzle with the recent action around the edges. A good history of science is, for the most part, an intellectual description of the dynamics of this road map, jigsaw puzzle-like structure as it has grown with time, first at one place, then in another. It is generally recognized that the process of solving the puzzle, of extending the road map, appears to be transnational and strategies are dictated for the most part by the opportunities provided by each scientific stage itself.

In other words the problem-seeking algorithm in science is not which is the next most useful problem to solve or how can we improve our exporting capability or how can we provide jobs but which is the next morsel that will help fill in the puzzle. Money with socially valuable potential is thus added to consumer prices or taxed away and given to the puzzle sawyers, in the process of which its socially valuable potential, while not completely filtered out, is made indeterminate. Only in the rare case where a timely social goal coincides with the next piece of the puzzle does the world profit from the private or public expenditures of one nation.

In contrast, monies given to professionals are targeted to express social goals. Also, professionals are further enjoined to use as little ammunition as possible. The process forces them to adopt a cupiscence for sharpshooting. If they use too many bullets the society that engages them will go to a more efficient practitioner. By the fact that society willingly and atomically pays their fees, professionals are by definition providing economically valuable services. Robert Harris ("Boot Strap Essence-Seeking", *JAE*, November 1975) refers to the professionals' *modus operandi* somewhat more poetically as "essence seeking" but the idea is the same: seeking essence is the same as sharpshooting in that both are in

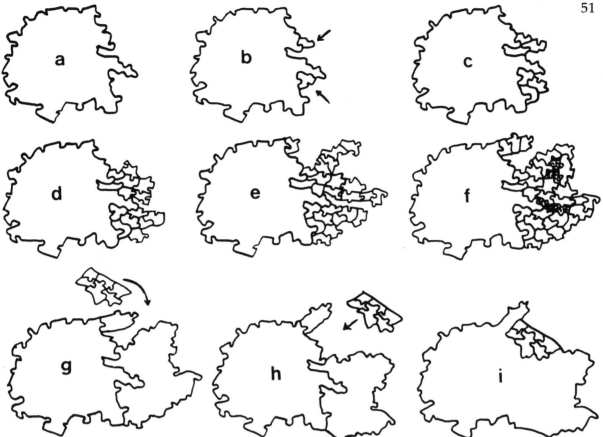

Jigsaw Puzzle Model of the way the growing corpus of scientific papers fits together. The model shows nine successive stages illustrating the tendency of action to develop where there is action already (**b–d**). It shows the way in which some areas may become contained and fill in rapidly (**e** and **f**) and how islands may develop and require a distortion of the original structure before they can be fitted neatly into place (**g–i**).

hot pursuit of value. The difference between the subset of professionals and the larger set of ones-who-do-technology is contained in the ancient rubric of *la profession libérale*: the professional, unless corrupted, works as a free agent for fees (not salary) and is historically obliged to subsume the paying client's goal into a larger social fabric.

Exactly how each profession works is (again, unless corrupted as some certainly now are) of no social or economic importance but may be of scientific interest. An interesting exceptive case is the investigation now ongoing at Pennsylvania State University through their Office of Continuing Education. They are trying to find out exactly how a variety of professions actually work in order to better provide them with continuing education services. Another one is John Myer and Richard Krauss' study of their own architectural office (1968) with an eye to computerization (available from the MIT Center for Building Research). Yet another is my own work for Mead Data Central for the same purposes (1981).

There is an isomorphism between scientific education and process as well. One marches through the MS, BS, and Ph.D. and continues straight up the drainage pattern until the spawning ground is reached. Except the pattern is not well-drained and researchers seldom if ever return to the sea. They spend their entire careers in these upper reaches, either win their Nobel* prize or not, and never learn anything of the work of not only the rest of the world but also of their scientific colleagues in nearby tributaries.

In emulating science, professional schools and, to a lesser extent, the entire rest of the university, have distorted themselves in ways that have serious long-term consequences. As the economics curriculum grew to include such 'scientific' material as econometrics (for anthropology, anthropometrics; for history, cliometrics) the FPD (first professional degree) inflated to a master's and, now, a Ph.D. Since the undergraduate is supposed to have his or her econometrics down cold on arrival in graduate school, it is *de facto* induced into the undergraduate career, as well as the support studies it prerequires. Students thus receive far less humanities and such rich amalgams as political economy have virtually ceased to exist. Recent events in Poland are therefore opaque to both political 'scientists' and economists but not to their predecessors of two generations ago who studied both.

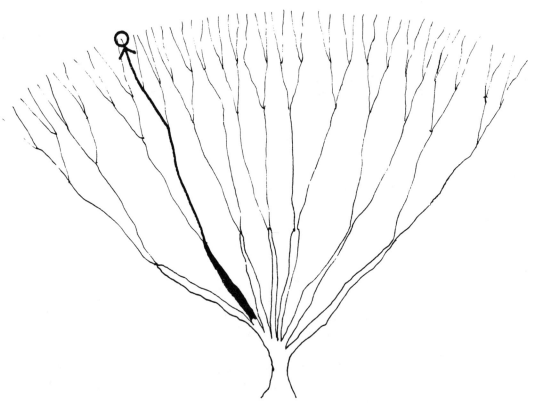

The natural progress of scientific investigation is dendritic and one-way from the mouth in morphology—ending up isolated in some far tributary.

---

*Alfred Nobel was a Swedish technologist who studied engineering in the U.S. Nitroglycerine had been around since 1846 when, working in his father's factory in 1864, he hit upon packing the unstable $C_3H_5 (ONO_2)_3$ in a safe absorbent, thus inventing dynamite. His patents made him one of the richest men in the world and he endowed the Nobel Prizes over his guilt regarding some of the uses of his invention. The laity have no hope of judging the validity of the academies' awards in science but I defy any well-educated person to identify over half the recipients in literature, a far more accessible field of endeavor.

Similarly, medical education* now begins in the first semester of high school. By the time students actually get to medical school they are surprised to find out that they are essentially in a research institution. A good portion of the faculty role models are life scientists, not clinicians. In neither economics nor medicine does one now learn anything about the society one is supposed to operate on. Finally, the U.C.L.A. Medical School hired literary personality Norman Cousins to teach humor to their students. The SIU School of Medicine has a supposedly remedial "Department of Medical Humanities." The pattern repeats itself again and again. The Ph.D. is rapidly replacing the Ed.D. in education as more research sociologists and psychologists are appointed. Schools of business management are filling up with applied mathematicians, operations researchers and mathematical programmers with a concomitant decrease of teachers, and education in, management practice. Tending to perpetuate their own credentials, the DBA is now proliferating and, to close the circle, is becoming the "terminal" degree required for business school teaching. Law schools have inflated their credential from a L.L. B. to a J. D., ostensibly so graduates can start at a higher pay scale in the government by virtue of holding a doctorate. Some institutions, and Yale Law stands out among them, have shown strong 'inter-disciplinary' tendencies, such as the desire to sit on pan-university Ph.D. committees, etc.

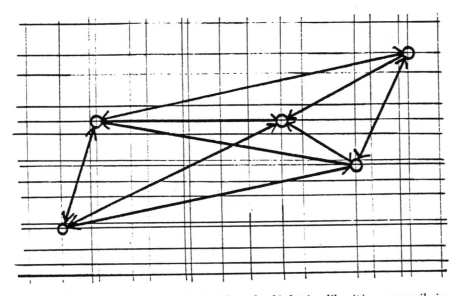

By contrast, the tendentious nature of professional method is lattice-like; it is necessarily in context and never far away from its innumerable sources of relevance.

*Medicine has its own battery of basic research funding agencies, such as the giant National Institutes of Health, the Air Force Institute of Pathology, the Center for Disease Control, etc. Even the Veterans' Administration hospital system, clear as its mandate is, has been moving heavily into basic medical research lately through closer liaisons with nearby medical schools and their faculties. There are, however, grounds for optimism as well. The currently on-going Muller-Kaiser Study of the AMA may, when it is finished, rival the Flexner Report of 1910 in its significance. Mr. Muller has publicly speculated on whether the present direction of medical education has had "the effect of dehumanizing the physician-to-be" and has encouraged early admissions to medical school as a way of encouraging pre-med students to take more humanities.

With the criteria for promotion and tenure of professional school faculty now fully coinciding in practice with those of the scholar/scientist, the distinction between these faculties will continue to disappear. Engineering will draw yet more of its faculty from physics and mathematics. In the near future, few professors of engineering will be professionally licensed or have industrial experience or interest, a scenario outlined by Eric Walker in the January 1978 issue of *Engineering Education*.

In "Civilizing Education: Uniting Liberal and Professional Learning" (*Daedalus*, Fall 1974), Martin Meyerson reminds us that until the age of 'Rationalism' universities were centers of professional education. All prepared for clerical and religious careers; Bologna and Salerno, coming into existence around the Millenium, started respectively as law and medical schools. Continuing, he points out an awful trend, one your author attributes to the scientization of the university:

> "It is not specialization or dedication to a discipline that is troubling. It is overspecialization. Many of the persons who are narrow experts today were more broadly cultivated than their present students. We live off this residue of broad knowledge now. The fields in which our eminent scholars work have expanded and been sub-divided so much, and the literature has so proliferated, that there is a narrower academic path to follow. The student today is not so fortunate as his sixty-year-old professor was when he was a novitiate."

I urge you to carefully consider what this means. It doesn't mean we are dealing with a reversible 'fad' in education, like "integrated liberal studies," or a boom and bust cycle, like the rush to sign up for law school in the seventies or engineering in the eighties. It means we are on a one-way street. When we want to go back we will not have the human capital to do it expeditiously.

Another, external, way to look at the situation is to examine the corporations' "make or buy" decision regarding education. That is, to what extent do American firms (1) feel the need at all for further education for their employees, and (2) if there is a felt need, to what extent do these firms buy it or make it (through creating their own institutions)? Throughout the fifties and sixties many corporations had liberal policies regarding release time and even funding for advanced education for their employees, to be purchased outside the company. National Training Laboratories President Harold Hodgkinson relates the more up-to-date case of Holiday Inns Inc., who approached several universities about a training program for their middle-management supervisors without luck. They finally built Holiday Inn University in Memphis. An even more revealing case was reported in the 17 July 1980 issue of the *Washington Post*:

> "Tyngsboro, Mass. . . . The Wang Institute, a graduate school in computer sciences named after one of the region's new breed of electronics moguls, Wang Laboratories Chairman An Wang, opens in September to help meet an acute industry-wide demand for budget-conscious software scientists.
>
> The problem with many academic institutions, say Wang and many of his corporate compatriots along "Hitech Highway"—Rte. 128 in Massachusetts—is that degree-fresh scientists are trained in traditional research theory and they often do not have the kind of practical bent a professional school could instill.
>
> 'I've been hearing complaints for years from managers who can't find people with the proper training to run projects,' says the Shanghai-

born, Harvard-educated Wang, whose family provided an initial endowment of nearly $3 million to begin planning the school more than a year ago.

"MIT is doing a good job locally, but they are more academic than professionally oriented,' he adds."

Furthermore, while recent figures show that 12 million adult Americans are studying inside the university system, there are now *48 million* studying *outside* of it. In 1979 AT&T spent $1.2 *billion* on in-house education, four times MIT's annual budget. If American colleges and universities wanted to supply this service clearly these revenues would be going to them. To the extent that foreign multinationals have their educational needs met directly with public funds our native firms are handicapped with additional expenses that lessen their ability to compete.

Yet another way to view the situation is through the decline of design. In the *Science of the Artificial,* (1969) a brilliant piece of proto-apostasy by Herbert A. Simon, he powerfully argues for saving design as the central function of professional activity:

"In view of the key role of design in professional activity, it is ironic that in this century the natural sciences have almost driven the sciences of the artificial from professional school curricula. Engineering schools have become schools of physics and mathematics; medical schools have become schools of biological science; business schools have become schools of finite mathematics. The use of adjectives like "applied" conceals, but does not change, the fact. It simply means that in the professional schools those topics are selected from mathematics and the natural sciences for emphasis which are thought to be most nearly relevant to professional practice. It does not mean that design is taught, as distinguished from analysis."

In 1560 Giorgio Vasari successfully petitioned Cosimo de Medici to found the *Accademia del Disegno,* thus marking the reemergence of the design professions. By 1980 Simon Ramo was writing in *America's Technology Slip:*

"Most higher education rarely plants the seeds to grow creative education, and when it does, little nourishment is applied to make it blossom. In engineering education the students spend most of their time working problem examples by the specific methods which have been explained in class and in the textbooks. They are taught prescribed ways to analyze certain situations and how to use a group of already developed analytical tools. All this is properly categorized as training in analysis, not synthesis or invention. The students not only fail to get an introduction to design—the finding of a practical, real-life solution to a bundle of requirements or performance, size, weight, appearance, and customer satisfaction—they also get no introduction to the concept of being innovative."

THE ECONOMICS OF SCIENTIZATION: STASIS

During the era of the U.S.'s most explosive technological growth, from 1875-1905, federal support for basic *and* applied research was virtually nil. The financial support came, in massive gushes, from the private sector. First we imported at trivial cost (postage, translation expenses, journal subscriptions) such basic research as was necessary. Then, through the public sale of stock, we raised the capital necessary for development and production. Since we were both research poor *and* capital poor, much of this investment came from abroad as well. If this sounds vaguely familiar, it is because this is exactly how the economies of

Japan, Korea and Malaysia proceed today. It is also the *modus operandi* of Germany, from whom the British and finally the U.S., ironically inherited the notion of the *Wissenschaft* University. France, long an imitator of Germany, has decided to eliminate the middleman and has publicly announced its intention to emulate Japan. Bear in mind that when we point out that the ratio of U.S. federal support for applied vs. basic research has shifted from 20:1 in Hoover's time to 7:5 in Reagan's we are speaking only of the circumscribed financial world of present and future (deficit) tax dollars. Consider instead that from Hoover to Reagan total federal funding for basic research increased from $10 million to $5,310,848,000 and for applied research from $200 million to $7,284,134,000 for a total of $12,594,982,000. This would put over 25 *million* youngsters through a year at my local junior college. For both categories summed this is an increase of 5998%. These are dollars that have not been available to Edison, Ford, Birdseye, Otis, or, for that matter, Edwin Land, Howard Head, or Steve Jobs. The money these innovators need is supplied by savers. The savings rate in the U.S. is 4%. The savings rate in Japan is 20%. You cannot save what is taxed away and spent on 'disinterested' research by DOD and NSF. Howard Head's 'interested' research produced the best selling tennis racket in Japan as did Steve Jobs' the best selling personal computer in the world.

Another measure is the marginal productivity of the scientific worker. Stephen Dresch of the New Haven Institute for Demographic and Economic Studies, who has also read Derek de Solla Price's work on the economics of science, comments as follows in the 16 March 1982 issue of the *Chronicle of Higher Education:*

> "Scientific genius, or even talent, is not uniformly distributed within the population. That is clearly indicated by Derek deSolla Price's findings that over half of the published scientific work of any generational cohort of scientists is contributed by the most productive 6 percent of the cohort's members, and that 20 percent contribute in excess of 90 percent of the generation's publications. Unless selection into and out of scientific careers is extremely random, it is highly unlikely that any given reduction in the number of people pursuing scientific careers would be translated into a corresponding reduction in scientific output. *At the economist's margin,* it is very likely that expansion or contraction in the scale of scientific activity has no significant effect on the rate of growth of scientific knowledge . . .
>
> But, even if most scientists contribute little or nothing to scientific knowledge per se, they might yet contribute to technology—to the utilization of scientific knowledge to achieve practical objectives. This assumes, however, that relatively (scientifically) unproductive scientists do devote themselves to technological applications of scientific knowledge. In fact, many do not, preferring to toil on the periphery of the real scientific action, and, over the postwar period, progressively more people were able to find support in academe for such unproductive scientific work . . .
>
> The problem in the 1950's, 1960's, and even (surprisingly) the 1970's, however, was that many of the students were being groomed not to enter the world of technology but to join the ranks of the generally not highly scientifically productive academic-science labor force."

Until very recently the number of scientists was small. There are now more scientists in England than clergy and military officers combined. If the present rate of increase continues, in 60 years everyone will be a scientist. It is not surprising to find that enormous public subvention has drawn the population into scientific work until the human factor of production of scientific knowledge has become the least rewarding factor to increase. Bertallanfy himself has noted that for many novitiates science has become a job rather than a calling. Besides numbers there is also disposition. Most scientists work in the public sector. Those who do not work for very large corporations. By and large, scientists are something large corporations can afford, like oriental carpets and limosines. Small companies, those which provide most new jobs, cannot afford them.

Yet when the factors of production for science increased right across the board and politicians notice little marginal increase in job-producing technology the scientists merely remark that we haven't quite spent enough yet. Skinflint Ronald Reagan requested $53 billion in research and development from Congress in February of 1984 for FY 1985, an increase of 14% over the year before.

THE ECONOMICS OF SCIENTIZATION: THE LONG RUN

History tells us international juries awarded British products most of the prizes for the hundred categories of manufacturers at the 1851 International Exhibition. Sixteen years later, at the 1867 International Exhibition held in Paris, British products received a bare dozen awards. The difference can be attributed solely to changes in education on the continent. With the British industrial revolution created outside the university and normal publication channels and with the export of British 'know-how' prohibited by law, the countries of the continent had to discover new technology on their own. By 1867 the job was done and Britain lost, never to recover, its industrial advantage even though it continued to blaze away for another century in basic research. The extent to which the continental Polytechniques and Technische Hochshulen wove in tendentious design, innovation and management is a telling point: it's not just capacity for research that is important but also the ability to translate it into saleable goods and services. U.S. professional education, by converting from the Land Grant model to the English model, has succeeded in ensuring the same economic disadvantage realized by the British.

As a result of WW I the American industrial plant was established but the U.S. continued its tradition as a substantial importer of basic science and advanced technology, which was adapted for domestic use through the technical expertise of the Land Grant universities and the nascent private R&D facilities of American firms and corporations. But with the advent of WW II the U.S. industrial plant was greatly extended and domestic basic research began to grow as fast as, and then much faster, than our applied technological capability.

According to MIT Vice President Kenneth A. Smith, American industry now supports only 3% of the research done at American universities. He also says that industry funding is unlikely to offset any reductions in federal funding. American University Professor of Technology and Administration Nanette Levinson surveyed 100 industry and university research directors in May of 1982. She reports that industry/university relationships are hampered by the "publish or perish syndrome", "anti-industry activists," and the "arrogant, superior attitudes of faculty." In the heyday of the Land Grant university private firms queued up to sponsor research; now the Government gives the schools grants on topics largely selected by themselves. "Thus, the industrial share of academic research funding declined from in excess of six percent in 1955 to about 2.5 percent in 1970, while the Federal share increased from 40 percent to 70 percent."

(Stephen P. Dresch "Intellectual Competence and the Circulation of the Elites: The Crisis of the late Twentieth Century", International Institute for Applied Systems Analysis "Working Paper," 1984. Quoted with permission of the author.) Apostate Kenneth Boulding now characterizes the U.S. as having a "grants economy."

Although folklore insists that the more money spent upon basic research, the better, there is considerable evidence to the contrary. During the 1970's the U.S. and Britain led the industrialized world in both Nobel prizes and trade deficits. Following the Post-War reconstruction period, England and the U.S. turned their attention with unqualified success to the further improvement of their basic research endeavors. From 1951-1976 the U.S. captured 59% of the Nobel science awards. In 1983 the U.S. won *all* the Nobel prizes in science. In the same period Britain led the world in Nobel prizes per capita. Japan, on the other hand, with hardly a Nobel laureate to its name, has taken a commanding trade position, as has Germany with its Nobel science awards now down to nearly one-third their pre-WW II level.

The redirection of higher education has had rather uniform effects upon the professions' performance in the U.S. In 1950, when the NSF was first funded, the U.S. ranked sixth in infant mortality. By 1967, the U.S. was winning 50% of the Nobel prizes in medicine and the life sciences but had dropped to eighteenth place for infant mortality and twenty-first for life span. Japan, with negligible contributions to medical science, has the lowest infant mortality and greatest longevity in the world. At the same time the cost of U.S. health services has risen to the point where it is questionable whether society can afford them. The confirmation of the U.S. medical schools as graduate research institutions and producers of specialists has also made the cost of medical education prohibitive. Today, approximately 50% of the physicians entering U.S. practice have been educated abroad. There are now more Thai doctors practicing in New York City than there are serving Thailand's rural population of 28 million.

In 1968 Britain was spending a higher percentage of its gross national product on R&D than any other country in Europe and yet it had one of the lowest economic growth rates. Japan, with less than half the British expenditures on R&D, had an economic growth rate that was three times that of the United Kingdom.

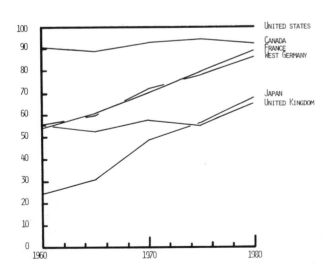

REAL GROSS DOMESTIC PRODUCT PER EMPLOYED PERSON FOR SELECTED COUNTRIES COMPARED WITH THE U.S.A.
(INDEX, UNITED STATES = 100)

England's inability to translate into an economic advantage the basic research that discovered radar, jet engines, antibiotics, etc., is being repeated in the U.S. Thus, in the period from 1947 to 1960, when the U.S. took a commanding lead in Nobel prizes for physics and our total national research expenditures tripled, the rate of economic growth dropped from 3.7 percent per annum to 3 percent. Between 1973 and 1975, the U.S. productivity rate actually declined in six out of seven consecutive quarters. In the first five years of the 1970's, the level of industrial productivity in Sweden rose 11 percent faster than ours, 17 percent faster in West Germany, and 24 percent faster in Japan. Western Europe and Japan are expected to maintain a better than 2 percent per year improvement edge over the U.S. in this decade. The inability of the English-speaking countries to provide a significant improvement in their productivity over the past sixteen years is clearly shown in the accompanying graph, from the Department of Labor's Office of Productivity and Technology.

Further, productivity and GNP per capita are closely related. At the close of WW II, the U.S. led the world in GNP per capita. By 1977 we were in fifth place; just three years later we were in eighth place as West Germany, Belgium, and Norway passed us. West German GNP/Capita is now 10% greater than ours. Also, retained GNP may be invested in ways that, although substantial, do not increase productivity. Robert Brown's unpublished, "Prospect for the 80s: A Study of Soviet-American Education and Technical Development," shows that while both the USSR and the U.S. make substantial investments in physical plant, much of it is repair and replacement rather than innovative substitution that increases productivity.

In 1964 the U.S. enjoyed a favorable trade balance of $7 billion which shrank to $4.1 billion by 1967. Ten years later that positive trade balance had steadily eroded to become a 1976 trade deficit of $5.9 billion which then ballooned to a negative balance of trade of over $26 billion in 1977. Arguments that the imbalance was aggravated by the high price of imported oil fail when one realizes that Japan, importing essentially 100 percent of its oil and raw materials, managed a world-wide trade surplus of over $16 billion in the same year.

Regarding invention, the U.S. patent balance declined almost 47% between 1966 and 1975 (see accompanying graph). This was due to the 91%

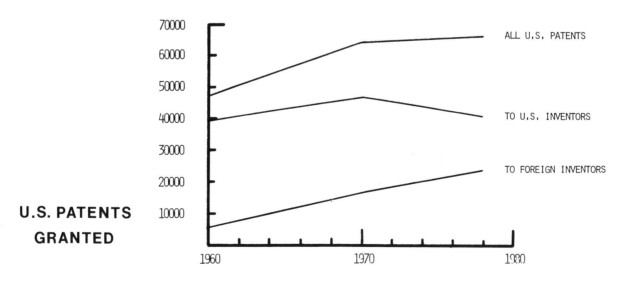

increase of foreign-origin patenting, coupled with a leveling off and eventual decline in the number of foreign patents awarded to U.S. citizens. The number of U.S. patents granted per year to U.S. inventors and corporations reached a peak in 1971 and has declined steadily since then. The number granted to foreign inventors has increased almost every year since 1963. The United States has a favorable but declining patent balance with Canada and six common market countries but a negative balance with West Germany and Japan. Thus the two countries most active in obtaining U.S. patents are West Germany and Japan. Since 1963, West German inventors have been granted the largest amount of foreign-origin patents, but Japan is fast approaching the West German level. Since 1970, Japanese patenting in the United States has increased more than 100 percent in almost every major industrial category.

The U.S. economic future looks quite bleak when our trade position is examined further. We find a pattern being repeated for product after product. At the end of WW II the excellent high voltage laboratories of two U.S. universities were replaced with a physics laboratory in one case and a linear accelerator in the other. Some ten years later much of the advanced extra high voltage transmission technology used in the U.S. was being imported from Sweden. Chronic trade balance weakness appeared in at least 122 manufacturing industries such as steel, paper, leather, glass, textiles, apparel, shoes, shipbuilding, autos, watches, and sporting goods. In 1966, these 122 industries provided 35% of the nation's industrial jobs, but ran up a hefty $7.5 billion trade deficit. In 1980, Japan produced three million more automobiles than the U.S. and it appears that Isuzu has developed a marketable adiabatic diesel, even though the basic research was done here.

The last decade has not improved our manufacturing posture. In spite of the U.S. invention of the transistor and an overwhelming commitment to basic solid state research, we have not been able to sustain a consumer electronics industry. The last U.S. television manufacturer has given up its U.S. plants. The lack of correlation between a nation's basic research ability and its prowess in the marketplace has been dramatically illustrated in a study by U.S. Commerce Department economist Michael Boretsky published in the 22 May 1978 issue of *Fortune.* Although the U.S. made 17 out of the 18 major breakthroughs in semiconductor electronics between 1947 and 1974, our exports in electronics and communications went from $300 million surplus in 1965 to $2 billion deficit in 1977.

Loss of the consumer electronics market leaves the U.S. dominant in only agriculture, chemicals, computers, and aircraft. However, even these positions are not secure. A government financed European consortium has produced the Airbus to challenge U.S. aircraft manufacturer(s). A French company recently sold a substantial fleet of helicopters to the U.S. Coast Guard. Also, we face steadily increasing Japanese competition for the international computer market. At the beginning of the 1970's, the Japanese Ministry of International Trade and Industry (MITI) concluded that "The Computer Industry is the future money-earner of Japan." MITI grouped six major Japanese companies with the leading engineering schools into three development ventures and over five years contributed some $225 million in applied research and development subsidies. The program paid off in the development of a new series of computers that has helped cut IBM's market share in Japan. Currently, MITI is spending $1.25 billion over four years to develop the next generation of very large scale integrated circuits for the computer industry. MITI houses a division to translate science and technology journals (predominately from English) and buck slip them to companies that could possibly profit from them. As Peter Drucker has observed (*Science,* May 25, 1979) "It is not true . . . that a modern developed country needs a science base. It can purchase it or import it." Fairchild Camera and Instrument executives state that their industry is now competing with "Japan, Inc." and report that the Japanese have made no bones about the fact that they want to be the IBM of the world in the 1985-90 time frame.

Our growth at the margin in agricultural productivity is decreasing. In architecture and civil engineering, the December 1979 issue of *Engineering-News Record* reports that from mid-1978 to September of 1979 (a little over a year) the U.S. share of the Middle East construction market dropped from 10.3 percent to 1.6 percent, for a balance of payments loss of over $80 billion. *Engineering-News Record* ranked the Koreans as first in contracts won and the U.S. as 12th. A *Washington Post* commentary of 29 November 1979 points out that the Korean contractors were trained by the U.S. Army Corps of Engineers during the 1950's.

Education is not the only cause of all this trauma. There are numerous other frequently offered reasons for the vitiation of U.S. productivity such as beggar-thy-neighbor trade policies (both given and received); a lack of foreign policy considerations in domestic decision-making; excessive regulation, inflation, and tax policies which steal away the retained earnings that support investment. As well, there is the entrance into the labor force of the untrained (war babies) and the less qualified (the disadvantaged), accompanied by a precipitous decline in SAT scores across all sex, race and income levels variously attributed to television, relaxed home and school discipline and the decline in verbal skills caused in turn by the decline in foreign language study. The SAT factors mentioned are from *On Further Examination,* the College Entrance Examination Board Advisory Panel Report of 1977, which lists all those reasons and more but deliberately refrains from anything sterner than noting that the average break-even point between hours of TV viewing and classroom attendance occurs late in a child's sixteenth year.

While this is all well known the contributing factor of the scientization of educational structure has been totally ignored. Econometricians are able to explain away only ½ to ¾ of our disproductivity. It is very hard to quantify a culture shift. In addition, while several of the standard reasons as listed above could equally be causes as well as effects of vitiated productivity the shifts in education cannot be so considered. The weight of the consequences of our present modes of education are hard to evaluate except in the striking parallels with Britain. Britain had the *same advantages, such as the Marshall Plan, and few of the disadvantages,* of its currently out-producing colleagues of Germany, France, Italy, Japan, Korea, etc.

THREE CASES

All three cases come to us from M. Ways' "The Road to 1977" in the Australian F. E. Emery's *Systems Thinking* (1969):

> "The history of the new style is well known. From scattered beginnings as 'operations analysis' in World War II, it coalesced as an institution in the postwar Rand Corp., which did analytical work in the systematic comparison of weapons for the Air Force. Through the fifties, this mode of presenting alternatives to decision makers had an increasing

influence on the Defense Department. Beginning in 1961, Secretary Robert S. McNamara restructured the whole work of the department in this style, programming all planning and procurement around missions or objectives that cut across the boundaries of the three services and extended beyond the confines of annual budgets. (For purposes of congressional appropriations, the programs are translated into conventional annual budget terms by means of 'crosswalks'.) This way of administering the Defense Department proved so successful that in 1965 President Johnson directed that PPBS (planning-programming-budgeting system) be introduced into all departments of the federal government. The new techniques have been helpful in foreign-aid planning and in defining Peace Corps missions. They are beginning to be recognized as the greatest advance in the art of government since the introduction nearly a hundred years ago of a civil service based upon competence. The new style, indeed, corrects an old defect of bureaucratic organization, which was at its best when performing routine tasks, at its worst in innovating and generating forward motion.

Business schools and corporate planners began developing the new technique at about the same time as the Rand Corp.'s early work for Defense. Since then the efficiency of the new methods has been brilliantly demonstrated in the marketplace. As Arjay Miller, president of Ford Motor Co., has put it: 'Hunches and cut-and-try' [Note: management 'scientists' are fond of pejorative terms for professional method. Other commonly used terms are "seat of the pants" or "rule of thumb."] methods are giving away to the systems-analysis approach, a whole new way of perceiving problems and testing in advance the consequences of alternative actions to solve those problems. Computers and other technical devices, including mathematical models, have extended greatly our ability to understand and cope with the complex problems we face in today's world.' "

Case I: While operations research may have won World War II they did so from contained advisory units. The sensitivity of problems was largely determined by seasoned warriors and it was to professional warriors that the analytical results were reported. It is equally arguable that operations research and systems analysis lost the war in Vietnam. Gaming strategies that implicitly assumed Western mentalities in our European and largely Westernized-Japanese enemies did not work against the "inscrutable" Viet Cong. Our scientifically developed machine carbines were no match for the Viet Cong's homemade weapons. Our 'simulated conditions' were in Aberdeen, Md.; their weapons were not 'simulated' at all but were developed under actual battle conditions. But most importantly, the war was run by McNamara's researchers at the Pentagon rather than by professional warriors. Anyone with a serious question about how this war was fought is recommended to the attitude expressed in James R. Schlesinger's "Quantitative Analysis and National Security" in the January 1963 issue of *World Politics*. The survivors ignored such idiocy and fought the Viet Cong in independent guerilla bands. The rest, both rank and file, were either thoroughly demoralized or thoroughly dead.

Case II: While Johnson's civilian operations researchers were applying new techniques to the detailed level of government operations no one was attending to the pattern level. Thus the Wars on Poverty and Vietnam were blithely, and expensively, pursued without a thought of who would pay for either or when. All enthusiasm for efficiency and cost-cutting was at the level where the algorithms worked: pencils, desks and bullets. Research and development, as usual, were defense related which *over* stimulated a small segment of the economy. Military 'innovation', as usual, did not readily translate into the consumer goods economy. Raising taxes for the war was inconsistent with eradicating poverty. No one watched the 'big picture', which ultimately caused the inflationary Depression lasting from 1974 to the present, with no end in sight. Again, OPEC cannot be blamed since we are only 70% dependent on foreign oil and 100% dependent economies did much, much better than America during the period under question. Through the calumnious posturing of the economists' search for permanent scientific truth, instead of dynamic policy making, we have Nixon simultaneously declaring himself a "Keynesian" and doing what Lord Keynes *would never have done:* stimulating during expansion. Cases I and II are of special interest because empiricist approaches to either solving problems, maintaining stasis or managing a dynamic process are ideally suited to the way the bureaucratic game is played. The very first rule (just the opposite of the professionals' first rule) is to never take responsibility for anything. Setting up a complicated set of algorithms that no elected official has any hope of understanding is ideal for this. If something goes wrong it's not your fault but the system's—never mind who concocted it. I refer you now, with new dread, to the Bateson quote that begins this chapter.

Case III: Ford lost 1½ billion dollars in 1980 and 1 billion in 1981. It's bond ratings dropped to the Bs. It is generally recognized that if Ford had not been buoyed up by its Common Market earnings and it's cash cushion it would be out of business today. It's hard to tell with all its tax credits being drawn down but Ford may well have lost $2½ billion on their North American sales in 1980. So much for Arjay Miller's mathematical models. The general Post-War algorithm taught in business schools is to increase the value of the stock. This made sense for the fifteen to twenty years it took for our international competitors to rebuild their physical plant. Consumers world-wide had little choice then except to buy American goods. Note that Ford paid out $312.7 million in dividends the year it lost $1½ billion and $144.4 million the year it lost 1 billion. One of the algorithms (the capital asset pricing model, if I remember correctly) has dividends as a factor in the equation. Ford Europe has survived, prospered, and bailed out its parent company because it grew up in a field of sane competitors. We can expect much worse as our national demographic trend takes away our seasoned, experienced businessmen who know something about their product line and increasingly replaces them with management 'scientists' who know the formulae to raise the short term value of their stock while destroying the long run viability of the company.

Finally, Percy Bridgman's 1927 *The Logic of Modern Physics* protests too much when he declares:

> "This reaction, or rather new movement, was without doubt initiated by the restricted theory of relativity of Einstein. Before Einstein, an ever increasing number of experimental facts concerning bodies in rapid motion required increasingly complicated modifications in our naive notions in order to preserve self-consistency, until Einstein showed that everything could be restored again to a wonderful simplicity by a slight change in some of our fundamental concepts. The concepts which were most obviously touched by Einstein were those of space and time, and much of the writing consciously inspired by Einstein has been concerned with these concepts. But that experiment compels a critique of much more than the concepts of space and time is made increasingly evident by all the new facts being discovered in the quantum realm. The

situation presented to us by these new quantum facts is two-fold. In the first place, all these experiments are concerned with things so small as to be forever beyond the possibility of direct experience, so that we have the problem of translating the evidence of experiment into other language. Thus we observe an emission line in a spectroscope and may infer an electron jumping from one energy level to another in an atom. In the second place, we have the problem of understanding the translated experimental evidence ... However, the growing reaction favoring a better understanding of the interpretative fundamentals of physics is not a pendulum swing of the fashion of thought toward metaphysics, originating in the upheaval of moral values produced by the great war, or anything of the sort, but is a reaction absolutely forced upon us by a rapidly increasing array of cold experimental facts."

On the contrary, it was just that: a *departure* from science into metaphysics; and if the Logical Positivists had been aware of anyone's methodology except their own, for instance the methods of literary analysis, they would have recognized the extra duty that Einstein's work was being put to as *symbolic*—as a symbol necessary to carry exactly the freight of "the upheaval of moral values produced by the Great War."

In the long run it's done some good, it's done some harm; and it is time to tell the difference. At the same time there has been some genuine *social* apostasy. As the accompanying chart (from the Human Resource Commission, National Research Council) shows, PhDs earned by men have been declining since 1972 across the board and in advance of what anyone might expect from demographic dynamics. Students vote with their lives and are excellent early indicators. PhDs earned by women are, in contrast, still rising but this is a catch-up surge attributable to the womens' movement rather than any acuity about economic futures. A chart of FPDs (first professional degrees) earned by women, if it were available, would reveal exactly that acuity rather dramatically. Women constituted 5.7% of the student body in architecture in 1968-69, 8.3% in 1972-73 and 26.5% in 1981-82.

The United States, in April of 1982, dropped its $2.3 million membership in the Vienna-based International Institute for Applied Systems Analysis. The British, in July of 1982, dropped their $400,000 membership.

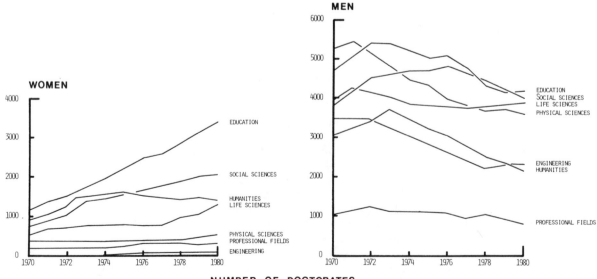

NUMBER OF DOCTORATES

The crux of my argument is simply this: although either of these two views, the many-value view, or the one-value view, could be all right in theory, in practice it turns out that the one-value view leads to results, and allows us to go deeper and deeper into what we are doing, while the many-value view, leads to a lot of words, and simply does not help us to reach better deeper results: in building, planning, or managing the environment. I should like to make it clear, at this stage in the argument, that I believe the many-value view, the neo-positivistic view, is extremely widespread in the world today, especially in academic circles, and that it has arisen precisely as the scientific world view has met, collided with, the need to design things, which is an activity not covered in any obvious way by science.

Christopher Alexander
"Value", *Concrete*, Vol. 1, No. 8, 1977

"MODERN" ARCHITECTURE: WITTGENSTEIN AND LOOS

Semi-apostate A. J. Ayer, in his *Philosophy in the Twentieth Century*, 1982, recounts that Wittgenstein was born in Vienna in 1889 of a Jewish descent family of wealthy industrialists who had converted to Christianity. After studying engineering at Berlin and Manchester he moved to Jena to study the philosophy of mathematics with Frege, who subsequently advised him to study with Russell at Cambridge, which he did from 1912-13. He was off and on a homosexual and wrote tormented letters to Russell over the "purity" of their friendship from the year 1913 to the outbreak of WW I from the isolated hut he had built in Norway. He came out of seclusion in 1914 and joined the Austrian army. He was taken prisoner by the Italians and assembled his *Tractatus* in prison camp. He wanted to discuss the manuscript with Russell after his internment but had given away his fortune after having read Tolstoy and couldn't afford the trip. Russell raised the money by selling Wittgenstein's furniture, which had been stored in Cambridge. From 1920 to 1926 he taught in village schools south of Vienna, a period ended by a legal action over his physical severity with the school children. He then spent a short time in a monastery, finally returning to Vienna to design a house for his sister in collaboration with his old friend, the civil engineer Paul Engelmann (from 1933 to 1938 Wittgenstein was listed in the Viennese city directory as an architect, not as a philosopher). It was during this period in the twenties that Wittgenstein associated with the Vienna Circle. In 1929 he returned to Cambridge and received his doctorate with Russell and Moore as examiners. From then until his death from cancer in 1951 he divided his time between England, his principal residence, and Vienna, with occasional hermitages in Norway and Ireland.

The house for his sister Gretl still exists in Vienna at Kundmanngasse 19 as the Bulgarian Cultural Institute and is the subject of but one monograph, Bernhard Leitner's *The Architecture of Ludwig Wittgenstein*, 1973. The house was designed and built between 1926 and 1928. Originally Engelmann was hired to prepare the plans. Wittgenstein was later asked in a letter from Gretl to help. Engelmann was a student of Adolph Loos and Engelmann and Wittgenstein worked together until Wittgenstein's fanaticism took over. Wittgenstein designed and had cast all the fittings: doors, locks, windows and even the radiators, which he had refused to use first go around and finally had cast overseas to his notion of perfection. In the beginning the plans were signed by both

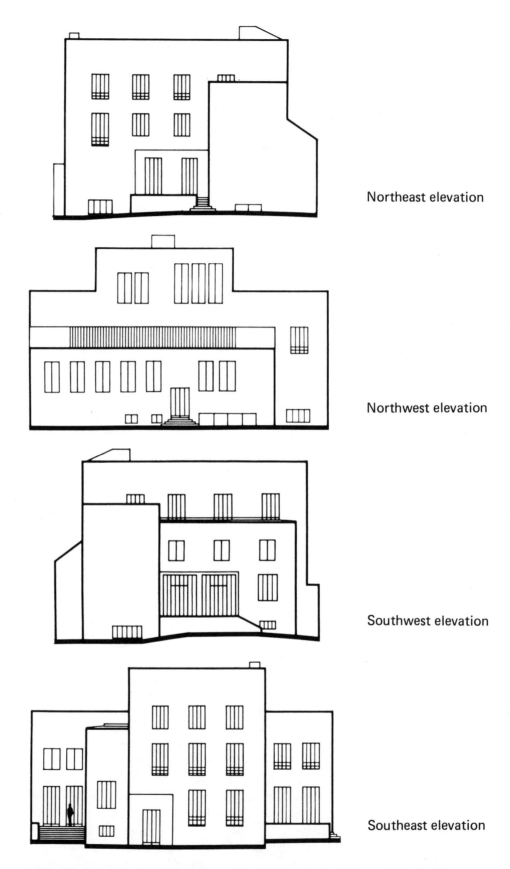

Northeast elevation

Northwest elevation

Southwest elevation

Southeast elevation

Villa Wittgenstein, Kundmanngasse 19, 1928. Ludwig Wittgenstein, Architect.

Wittgenstein and Englemann but all later plans were signed by Wittgenstein alone. The letters to vendors and manufacturers are in Wittgenstein's hand. After the house was finished he didn't like the proportions of a hallway and had the ceiling raised three centimeters. He also didn't like the way a stair came out and he entered a lottery hoping to win enough money to rebuild it. In her memoirs another sister, Hermine, called it a "house turned logic." In *Ludwig Wittgenstein, A Memoir,* 1966, Norman Malcolm states:

> "It is inside the unadorned building that its uniqueness becomes obvious. Georg Henrik von Wright writes that the beauty of this architecture, 'is of the same simple and static kind that belongs to a sentence of the *Tractatus'* . . . Wittgenstein's architectural language consists of only a few elements: [almost black] floors, light-colored walls and ceilings, metal doors and windows, and naked bulbs . . . Wittgenstein strictly rejected carpets, chandeliers and curtains—elements of interior decoration which are incompatible with the clarity and rigour of this architecture and its polished and precise surfaces. The way the few elements used by Wittgenstein are combined, and their thoroughly studied interconnecting proportions give the architecture of these spaces its nonsubjective, determined character."

We know of only two buildings by Wittgenstein and one was a primitive hut in Norway. The Villa, however, is the single most unrelenting statement of the ideals of "modern" architecture that has ever been built.

Adolf Loos studied architecture in Dresden until 1896, when he returned to his native Vienna where he stayed (except for three years in the U.S. spanning 1912-1914) until 1922, when he moved to Paris. While they both were exceedingly peripatetic there were times when both Wittgenstein and Loos were in Vienna together. In any case they knew of each other. Paul Engelmann was a student of Loos. Loos was in Vienna during the two most active decades of the Vienna Circle. He must have known of their work and very likely knew members personally. Wittgenstein certainly saw the design work of Loos and just as certainly read Loos' 1908 "Ornament and Verbrechen" (Ornament and Crime). It is with some irony that one reflects that the society of cafe conversation that permitted facile inter-professional conversation gave rise to a philosophy of "unity" that ultimately prevents it.

Wittgenstein's *ouvre* was miniscule, Loos' was not much larger. Loos was a devoted Anglo-and Americo-phile and had traveled widely in both countries, resulting in a discontinuous practice. Until the Villa Steiner of 1910 his work was all interior design, yet Loos' influence was enormous. Reyner Banham, in his article "Adolf Loos: Ornament and Crime", 1957, documents how Erich Mendelsohn and Walter Gropius changed from designing decorated buildings to designing undecorated buildings after reading "Ornament and Crime", and how Le Corbusier stole its anthems for his own writings. The timing is also consistent with Mies van der Rohe's shift. These abrupt shifts crystalized not into a *Wiener Kreis* discussion group but into a whole school: the Bauhaus at Dessau, Germany, whose war cry was the *Neue Sachlichkeit,* which Andrew Saint (*The Image of the Architect,* 1983) renders as "the new scientific objectivity." Saint also notes that founder Gropius "was really preoccupied from the start with an architecture created in the old manner but offering a rational appearance." The Bauhaus was closed under political pressure by the Nazis in the thirties. Half the faculty went to Russia and the other half scattered around the world, with key figures Gropius and van der Rohe taking over ITT and Harvard respectively. According to Turpin

Bannister's *The Architect at Mid-Century,* and the experience of several generations of architects, including your author, by 1954 the AIA regarded the imported Bauhaus curriculum as orthodoxy for American schools.

Thomas Wolfe (*From Bauhaus to Our House,* 1981) was right in that "modern" architecture, that is, architecture shorn of decoration, was a European import. We have now seen that the impetus of the new empiricism was also a European import. Indeed it came not just from Europe, but from Vienna, and from the same small time frame as well. But Wolfe was wrong in saying that "modern" architecture rose because of its most common building type, worker housing. That is much like saying that America's large cars appeared because they were sedans or convertibles or whatever rather than because of Eisenhower's defense highways, which demanded land cruisers. "Modern" architecture rose for exactly the same reasons that Logical Positivism rose—and at the same time and from the same *Umwelt.* By the end of the 19th century decoration had suffered the same loss of reputation that metaphysics had; neither were any longer capable of explaining the world or anchoring it against decay and decadence.

Here we must separate the notions of functionalism and rationalism, a task in which we are greatly aided by Dennis Sharp's *The Rationalists* of 1978. "Decoration" has not always had a pejorative connotation and, further, only in modern times has it become non-functional. Indeed, it was perfectly functional until the Industrial Revolution. Craftspersons since ancient times combined design and manufacture in a subcutaneous process that admitted such decoration as had *meaning* to the craftsperson himself, the user and the chance beholder. With the Industrial Revolution came a separation between the designer and the manufacturer. Decoration then became divorced from meaning as 1) it was used to "mask" mass production; 2) it could be more easily and cheaply produced, e.g., cast instead of carved; and 3) the sensibility of the united designer/manufacturer was gone. Decoration became a meaningless swirl that proliferated seemingly without end. *Art Nouveau* rose briefly as a reaction against Victorian encrustation on the premise that its forms were natural, from nature, and that nature was inherently meaningful. The earlier Arts and Crafts movement in England combined that ethos with a re-emphasis on the craftsperson and ended up producing goods only for the intellectuals and the rich.

Despairing of these failures to halt the dissolution of meaning in decoration, Adolf Loos gave up on tinkering with the syntax and threw out the language, just as the Logical Positivists, despairing of explaining or halting political, economic and moral denigration, threw out metaphysics. In both cases, the world was made simpler by artificially reducing the set of possible questions and actions. But the effect in architecture was not to make buildings more "functional" but to "rationalize" the taxonomy of *potential* functions to where all the difficult, subjective, social functions were gone. Indeed, in doing so architecture was made less, not more, functional. One is reminded of Russell's anecdote of church father Origen (*History of Western Philosophy,* 1946), written long after his empiricist apostasy. He recounts that Origen was tormented by his sexual urges after his vow of chastity and ended his torment with a sharp knife. Russell remarks that Origen did not *solve* his problem but simply *removed* it. Thus, in the earlier part of this century, did comprehensive movements in both architecture and philosophy (broadened to include sociology, psychology, economics, history and language) take similarly drastic and similarly irrevocable action.

An interesting side light is the changing role and development of architectural history. During the heyday of the "modern" movement, history was thrown out of consideration and curriculae as so much metaphysical baggage. Since all architecture of the past had decoration it was all bad. Everything had to be created anew and pure without the corruption of historical examples. When history edged back into the curriculum it was more often than not taught by architects rather than historians, and the formers' sense of history started with Loos. If they were determined to search for the "roots" of modern architecture they would show slides of 19th century iron bridges by British engineers. In the meantime, the *larger* wave of empiricism that enveloped the Post-War university did not miss the rejected and diminuitive specialty of architectural history. Rejected by the profession they existed to serve, architectural historians jumped at the chance to become scientific researchers rather than servitor-scholars. The "terminal" degree inflated to the Ph.D., which meant specialization. Thus a historian would come to know everything there was to know about the southwest pendentive of the northwest dome of Saint Front and be blind to its aura of Augustinianism. As the disciplines monasticized behind sequestering walls Wittgenstein went to the philosophy department and could not be in two places at once. As the custom of empirical verification took hold the work of an architect could not be examined unless there was a substantial body of work from which to extract evidence. G. L. Hersey writes in the preface to his *Pythagorean Palaces,* 1976:

> "I have written this book to establish the hitherto neglected fact that Italian Renaissance domestic architecture was largely ruled by Pythagorean principles. In recent generations of scholars, from Stegmann and Geymuller in 1885 to Heydenreich and Lotz in 1974, the historiography of Renaissance architecture has been in the hands of positivists—those who believe that knowledge is based only on physical objects empirically studied, and that meanings must be sought within the objects themselves. Their approach goes back to the nineteenth-century work of Auguste Choisy, who treated the history of architecture as an analogue to comparative zoology. From such a viewpoint there is little room for magic; rather, the achievement of this positivist school has been to classify styles of, and to reveal processes of, revival and influences."

Loos' small *ouvre* worked against him and by 1964 the renowned historian Nikolaus Pevsner (*Adolf Loos,* 1964), was able to write "Adolf Loos remains an enigma". It would be more properly stated that Adolf Loos had *become* an enigma through the transformation of architectural history that came neatly into place at that moment that modern architecture became old enough to study.

That "becoming" is, as Martin Meyerson enthymemes earlier in these pages, irrevocable at least in the short term because each generation's students since the War have had a less general foundation than the previous cohort. Our culture has relentlessly suffered reduction in spite of the "information explosion". The empiricists' concept of knowledge and inquiry has crystallized on the windows of our house and made them opaque, not just to history but also to the meaning of what we do now.

Speaking for architecture, a return to *meaningful* decoration as a commonplace is now at least three generations away. For over a quarter of a century it has not been considered necessary for an architectural student to learn to draw with a free-hand. Aside from the fact that this means that he or she has also not been taught to *see,* it also means that these architects are limited to such decoration as is easy to draw or for which there are templates. *Meaningful* decoration is another matter entirely. In the nineteenth century, when Thomas Hardy decided to be an architect, he did so by apprenticing to a well-known architect *after* sharing the same liberal arts education his mentor had. Thus each in turn had a grasp of the sort of civilization they were at every moment at the forward end of. Thomas Hardy could, and did, produce buildings with meaningful decoration. And, when the time came, he could also produce *Far From the Madding Crowd*. By 1977, none of the eleven authors in Spiro Kostof's *The Architect* believed that any architect's education of any era started until he either made the Grand Tour, matriculated into an *architectural* school, or apprenticed to this or that other architect. Yet these architects' ability to make decoration *meaningful* depended, as it would today, utterly on their knowledge of their countrymen and their culture, not of architecture *qua* architecture.

ARCHITECTURE AND MANAGEMENT SCIENCE

In the Post-War era the architecture client changed dramatically. Company founders retired. Business diversified for war production and rediversified for a transformed marketplace on return. As Eisenhower built his highways (as an anti-inflation measure to soak up dollars) new transportation and distribution algorithms* were demanded. Business, finance and management education were transformed by the new empiricism, whose methods mystified businessmen of one generation earlier.

Let us dwell for a moment on what the relationship must have been like between Mssrs. Carson, Pirie and Scott and Mr. Louis Henri Sullivan, their architect. Sullivan espoused both decoration and functionalism without contradiction. The relationship of Mssrs. Carson, Pirie, Scott and Sullivan was a professional one characterized by people communicating directly with each other about things they fervently cared about. The upshot is a precious and now historically valuable retail building that has been in continuous profitable operation for 80 years. The notion of "user needs" was not yet in existence in a strictly architectural context (but it certainly was in a social-economic sense) because all four men as individuals had their personal names and reputations at stake. Their names were on the building. Thus the "cost" of ornament, spacious aisles, numerous restrooms, and pleasant changing rooms was not thought of as a cost passed on to consumers but as a cost *of doing business,* something you paid *to be* in business. I present this paradigm not as unfamiliar material but because it matches perfectly the public's image of what the architecture/client relationship is like today—but hasn't been since before World War II.

Now let us examine another and admittedly not comparable business/architecture case, but one that is full of the ethos of the later twentieth century. Howard Head developed a metal ski after the war working in a garage large enough to support the huge overhead machinery necessary to static test materials. Architect unknown. His revolutionary ski was a huge success and sold

---

*These systems, based in linear programming, are what have brought you rock-hard, gassed tomatoes out of season and forbade you (in my area) apples in season from twenty miles away. After a near fatal quarter of a century assault, farmers' market are making a confused but welcome comeback. The same systems also brought you long chains of franchised fry pits and motels and has generally rendered the United States a place where one tours by automobile only under total lack of option. Regional differences and flavor have been all but wiped out since 1950, Calvin Trillin's charming but romantic books nonwithstanding.

all over the world. As an engineer and not a businessman he hired some managers to do those business-type things for which he had no enthusiasm. Having learned about latent assets, one of them suggested a line of sportswear emblazoned with "Head Ski." The quality of his skis had made his name valuable, and providing the sportswear didn't devalue his name, he was not adverse to the new profits. Systems were set up to control inventory, production, cash flow, etc., and marketing people pretended to know that each person in the U.S. would soon own .001 Head nylon shells. Meanwhile, Rossignol's French fiberglass skis knocked Head skis off their perch. That's when Head sold the company to AMF for $16 million. Surely his managers had suggested in that time marketing a tennis racket made in Taiwan with Head's name on it; but this wasn't sportswear, it was serious equipment. Thus, with his inventive time now freed, Head devoted himself to developing a better tennis racket. From more garage tinkering (but with better machinery) came the Prince racket, now the best selling racket in the world. Head is now twice retired.

During his career Head knew few of his ultimate customers and while many buildings had been built and used in making these skis, jackets and rackets, no customers can name any of their architects. It cannot even be said with any surety that Mr. Head could. Indeed, it is more than likely that the "client" for all these buildings consisted of a group of Head's managers including the vice president of operations, the vice president of finance, the facilities manager and the company attorney—none of them equity owners. The only concern for aesthetics likely surfaced at a cocktail party where the architect got to see the house of the vice president of operations, which was decorated by his wife, whose favorite color was aubergine. Given such a committee, decision-making criteria quickly iterate to their only common tongue: the quantitative. This is to be expected in a milieu where everyone has separate specialities and responsibilities and no one has a care for the organic whole.

But, you rightly ask, what of retailing, where environment and direct consumer meet? Can any reader name the architect of their nearest Penney's, Wards or K-Mart? Can you even recall what the building is like? Do you have the vaguest idea where the bathrooms are or whether the facility even has any? The firms that prospered in the Post-War era were the firms that designed these Penneys, Wards and K-Marts, as well as the high schools, junior colleges and everything else. These buildings are shorn of ornament, which ultimately had a salutory short-term effect on the bottom-line. No living individuals' names are on these buildings.

Another historic example is the worker housing built by George Pullman for the workers of the Pullman Palace Car Company in Pullman, Illinois. I illustrate this because it is less familiar architecture than the Carson Pirie Scott store and because it is a 19th Century American example of what Thomas Wolfe has based his entire *From Bauhaus to Our House* on. I am the last person to defend Pullman's paternalistic treatment of his workers and the wage cut of May 1884 (even though the prices of all goods fell every year from 1873 to 1883) that precipitated Eugene Debs' strike, which ended only with Grover Cleveland's federal troops occupying the town. Nevertheless, the worker housing was darn nice: solid construction, spacious, not niggardly detailed at all and, in general, far more commodious and rich in associative texture and detail with what the public considers "houseness" than any of the worker housing provided by modern movement architects. Thomas Wolfe neglected or didn't know of Philippe

Worker housing by the Pullman Palace Car Company, Chicago, Illinois.

Boudon's *Lived-in Architecture* (1969), a diary of Le Corbusier's worker housing in Pessac, France. It shows the slow transformation to the present of the village as workers added pitched roofs to their boxy shapes and window detail and balconies to their flat exterior walls in their inexorable pursuit of "houseness." The worker housing of Pullman had "houseness" right out of the carton and, indeed, is architecturally indistinguishable from Georgetown (District of Columbia) houses selling for a quarter million dollars each, both about the same distance from their downtowns.

Let us now compare this to another kind of worker housing where the landlord was not a robber baron but rather a benevolent city agency acting in good faith effort to produce low-income housing. I refer to St. Louis' infamous Pruitt Igoe housing project of which the world does not need another photo of falling down, as it did from the demolitionists' dynamite in 1975 after a mere twenty years of use and a not mere $57 million cost. Many reasons have been put forward for the project's failure, but none are so persuasive as the thorough-goingness of the empiricism of the architects, Helmuth, Yamasaki and Leinweber (not Skidmore, Owings and Merrill as stated in Martin Mayer's *The Builders* of 1978). First of all, being designed in the empiricist style it had no "houseness." Probably more important were such innovations as skip-stop elevators. With a certain mathematical elegance, the single elevator per building only stopped at the fourth, seventh and tenth floor, thus forcing a third of each elevator's passengers to each walk down either one, two or zero stories. That's not much to walk (if the elevator was working) and think of the savings! But the empiricists never put themselves in the place of an eight-year old on the playground with a full bladder; one for whom

all the buildings and all the entrances and all the elevators looked alike and who
never left the playground until he or she really had to. Once the elevators and
corridors were rank with urine the building was through, not as a necessary but
certainly as a sufficient condition. What happened to Mssrs. Helmuth, Yamasaki,
Leinweber and Head's accountants, architects and clients alike, was clearly
prophesized by John Dewey in *Art as Experience* (1934):

> "Compartmentalization of occupations and interests brings about separa-
> tion of that mode of activity commonly called 'practice' from insight, of
> imagination from executive daring, of significant purpose from work, of
> emotion from thought and doing."

What happened was that a management "style" was developed by some architects that matched the management "style" of the new empiricist business
managers. There was substance to it, such as the development of PERT schemes to
organize work better, computer programs in structural and mechanical design,
and the algorithms mentioned in both chapter one and earlier in this chapter, but
by and large the new management "style" was not very different from the new
architectural "style" in that it simply chose to pay attention to some things and not
others. This "no nonsense" approach affected the design of architects' offices and
their dress code as well. Tweed went out and chalk-striped flannels came in. While
their designs had no decoration their offices had less. The visiting vice president
for finance was impressed by this sense of economy and the corporate attorney
was impressed by the lack of attractive nuisances that spelled liability (but Wolfe is
quite right in that as soon as the building was finished these clients had their inner
sanctums furnished in expensive antiques). These architectural offices became the
big successful firms of the 1950s, sixties and seventies. Firms that remained rigged
for the proud proprietor with an expansive sense of care for the whole operation
and a concern for their customers' and employees' welfare became small, marginal
offices.

ARCHITECTURAL SCIENCE: THE EMPIRICISTS SAVE US FROM EMPIRICISM

Architecture and mathematics and science have a long intertwined history
that dates to the resuscitation of the academies. The word *accademie* reappears in
Italy after some Greek scholars went to Italy in 1438-39 in connection with a
scheme to reunite the Greek and Roman churches. The first academy involving
architecture that we have substantial documentation for is Vasari's *Accademia del
Disegno* in Florence, for which he received both social and fiscal warrants from
Cosimo de Medici on 13 January 1563. Indeed, we have the By-Laws (Biblioteca
Nazionale). Cosimo and Michelangelo were made the Capi, uniting prince and
architect. There were two profound reasons for founding these academies, both
well established in the literature. One was to give re-birth to the Ancients' way for
doing things and the other was to slip architects *into* the back door of the pantheon
of the humanities and *out* of the guilds.

On the first point there is no evidence to suggest that architects were anything
but professionals in ancient Greece. There is no record of their participation in the

philosophical academies nor of their being organized into a trade or guild. As Clarence Glacken says, in *Traces on the Rhodian Shore*, 1967,

> "It has been said by many that Greek science, unlike modern science, did not lead to the control of nature but the occupations, crafts and the skills of everyday life were evidences that changes were possible that either brought order, or more anthropocentrically, produced more orderly accessibility to things men needed. If by control over nature one means its modern sense, the application of theoretical science to applied science and technology, there was no such control in the ancient world. Conscious change of the environment need not, however, rest on complex theoretical science, as we well know from Roman centuriation. The power of mind was acknowledged in the analogy of the creator-artisan and in its potentials for rearrangement of natural phenomena, such as in the establishment of a village, the discipline of animals by men, the indirect control over wildlife with weapons, snares, and the like."

We do have, as always, their work; and the concept and application of *entasis* (for example) gives us insight into the orientation of the architects of ancient Greece. *Entasis* is a swelling of column, inclination of end columns, or curving of stylobate to correct the slight fish-eye vision of the human eye, especially as one comes closer to an object. The interesting aspect is that while *entasis* is a fairly subtle analysis and application of optics (mathematics and science) its sole meaning and purpose is human-based: correcting perception. That strikes this author as a very "professional" thing to do. The *concept* of *entasis*, however, eluded early Renaissance architects [the real scholarship (and larceny) was done in the 19th century by the English and Germans]. Renaissance architects stumbled around ancient ruins like men from Mars and mistook the *use* of mathematics for architecture's *meaning*. Thus the Renaissance was occupied wholly with unlocking the mathematical "secrets" of ancient architecture and, failing to do so, simply started inventing their own. This misconception still haunts us today and can be clearly seen in the current works of Portaghesi, Hedjuk, Eisenman and many others. Besides the actual work we also have the late Hellenistic Vitruvius' *De architectura* (c. 75 B.C.), a practical, lore-filled treatise that speaks to us over its two thousand years much more directly on professionalism than any of the mumbo-jumbo written in the Renaissance.

The second point is related but had principally to do with the social position of the newly re-emerging profession of architecture. The humanistic pursuits of philosophy, literature, mathematics, music, etc. were already well-established during the Middle-Ages while artists and painters were mere craftsmen organized into guilds (trade unions). Architects were either masons who rose to direct other masons (still as craftsmen) or they were humanist clients (clerics or merchant/banking princes) who sometimes verbally and sometimes graphically explained what they wanted done to the masons. Vasari made passionate petitions through his *Accademia* to be recognized as humanists, not as craftsmen, because while they did a certain amount of work with their hands the "essence" of their work was with their brains.* "Disegno," which meant either design or drawing, was according to Vasari an *espressione dichiarazione del concetto che sia nell' animo*. The appeal was particularly focused on mathematics because

---

*Interestingly, Da Vinci's earlier Academy (c. 1498) in Milano sought to include architecture and painting but *not* sculpture, as it was too dirty and sweaty a job. With Michelangelo as a Capo this didn't seem to be a point worth bringing up to Vasari.

they (wrongly) thought it constituted the central meaning of ancient architecture and because mathematics were already securely in the pantheon to which they wanted entrée. They got in. Vasari's academy gave lectures in mathematics and physics, the architects burned their guild cards, their social rank levitated, they started taking honoraria, fees and "keep" instead of prices or wages, and education began to take its place alongside apprenticeship. Architecture became learnéd.

Thus we are told that Alberti, Filarete, and especially Marsilio Ficino and Guarino Guarini were all accomplished mathematicians. There were also those who were scientists as well, such as the British Roger Joseph Buscoviach and Christopher Wren, who also held a professorship in astronomy. This was more likely in Britain than elsewhere or earlier because architecture, the military and science were about the outer limits of what an English gentleman could pursue. If you could only be either, one would expect some incidence of combinations. Wren is perhaps the only architect to have a feature-length article written on his architectural work in *Scientific American.* An even more astonishing fact regarding this particular "ghost in the machine" as it glides through the centuries occurs during the age of Rationalism that gave us Comte, Saint-Simon and finally Logical Positivism—and it comes to use from our most Francophilic President and the only one who claimed to be an architect: Thomas Jefferson. He proposed in 1814 to found a school of architecture at the University of Virginia but gave it up when he could not find a suitable *mathematician* to be its head. Thus, the U.S. had to wait 51 more years for M.I.T. to open its School of Architecture in 1865 as the first English-speaking university-based school of architecture in the world (the University of Liverpool won the race in the U.K. in 1894).

Thus we should not be wholly surprised by the three waves of empiricism in architecture. In the third wave there were two motions; one of architects and architecture historians going to science (as in the *Wiener Kreis*) and the other of their coming to us. In general, the former came first. In 1946 the German Sigfried Giedion (*Space, Time and Architecture*) rewrote architecture history under the influence of the general theory of relativity.* Why a paradigmatic shift in physics should change architecture anymore than it should affect the recipe for *coq au vin* is one of those mysteries that shall never be adequately explained but as of 1975 "ST&A" was the *only* book on the theory of architecture to appear by name in the U.S. national NCARB registration examination. Similarly, in the sixties the Greek Konstantine Doxiades tried to found the "Science" of Human Settlements, reaching his high point in 1969 when Norbert Wiener wrote the dust jacket notes for one of his books. Then there is Buckminister Fuller, also a charismatic figure of the sixties, who played the role of Otto Neurath but without the support and comfort of a gifted and profound circle. Other, more authentic scientists, were more like innocent bystanders. Thus when E. T. Hall's *The Hidden Dimension* appeared in 1966 he was co-opted by architects who imagined Hall to be inventing theory, somehow racked into *partis,* specifically for them. The second motion is the more interesting and serious: when the scientists (or architecture graduates with a decidedly scientific outlook) came to us.

---

*Which deserves quotation of the eloquent statement of apostasy by Dutch architect Aldo van Eyck, 1962: "By virtue of what memory and anticipation signify, place acquires temporal meaning and occasion spatial meaning. Thus space and time emerge humanized, as place and occasion."

Stirrings in environmental design research go back to the late fifties when some psychiatrists and psychologists began to realize that their wards were likely having negative effects on their patients. Key figures spanning this era are Osmond, Studer, Stea, Winkel, Gans, Sommer, Ittelson and Proshansky. An early text is *Institutional Neuroses* (1959) by the English psychiatrist Russell Barton. That stream joined the already existing momentum coming from the human factors/human engineering people. Then the Center for Building Technology in the U.S. National Bureau of Standards started up an architectural science section under John Eberhard's leadership in 1964. As "architecture" research their agenda differed sharply from the CBT's traditional "construction" research in materials testing. Eberhard later founded and directed the AIA's Research Corporation in 1973 and now is the Executive Director of the Advisory Board on the Built Environment at the National Academy of Sciences. The CBT Environmental Design Division was purged in 1981 partly by Reagonomics and partly (in fact mostly) because the physical scientists just didn't like the "soft" scientists. Another important early source of Federal support was the U.S. National Institute of Mental Health.

The patriarch of design methods science is Geoffrey Broadbent (*Design in Architecture*, 1973) of the Portsmouth Polytechnic in England. His sources are Shannon and Weavers' *The Mathematical Theory of Communication* (1949) and the work of the Ulm School of Design, the Hochschule für Gestaltung. In *Design in Architecture* Broadbent recounts,

> "By the early 1960s, systems engineering, ergonomics, operational research, information theory and cybernetics, not to mention the new maths and computing, were all available to the design theorist in highly developed forms, and several events marked the emergence of design methods from these sources as a discipline in its own right. This was seen most clearly at the Ulm School of Design . . ."

In some ways Ulm was the inheritor of the Bauhaus (long closed and anyway in East Germany) tradition but in other ways it wasn't. There was a thorough attempt at "analytical methodology" going on, pursued by the successive rectors of Otl Aicher, Tomas Maldonado and Herbert Ohl from 1962 to 1966. Broadbent also cites the appearance of engineer Morris Asimow's *Introduction to Design* (1962), the first of a series of books edited by Case Institute's James Reswick. Asimow's influential book was a welding together of the state of the art in systems engineering and information science. The middle sixties were years studded with numerous network-building conferences here and in England and with landmark issues of established periodicals dedicated to the emerging fields, such as Kates and Wohlwills' 1966 *Journal of Social Issues,* called "Man's Response to the Physical Environment" and Kenneth Craik's 1970 special issue of *New Directions in Psychology.*

Volume 1, Number 1 of the *DMG* (Design Methods Group) *Newsletter* was mimeographed in December of 1966 at the University of California/Berkeley Department of Architecture by Editor Gary T. Moore. There were then three Assistant Editors and an Editorial Board of fourteen people. Moore wrote: "The purpose of the *Newsletter* is to explore the general field of rational design . . . ." The first issue also announced the founding in September of that year of the Design Research Society in England. By March of 1968 the DMG *Newsletter* was being published by Sage Publications for the College of Environmental Design at UC/Berkeley. In 1969 the *Newsletter* mutated into a quarterly journal called *Design*

Theories and Methods, jointly sponsored by the U.S. DMG and the British Design Research Society. Around 1978 the latter started their own quarterly, *Design Studies,* ending the period of joint sponsorship of *Design Theories and Methods,* which now survives at Cal/Poly San Luis Obispo with sponsorship from the University of California/Berkeley Department of Architecture under the editorship of Donald P. Grant and J. P. Protzen with a circulation of 600.

The *Architectural Psychology Newsletter* started in the summer of 1967 at the University of Utah, under the editorship of John Archea. Archea had come as a student after Roger Bailey of the Department of Architecture and Calvin Taylor of the Psychology Department had secured a four-year NIMH grant to develop the first doctoral program in architectural psychology. Archea later moved to Penn State, taking the *Newsletter* with him and ultimately merging it into the *Man-Environment Systems* loose-leaf journal.

Volume 1, Number 1 of *Environment and Behavior* came out in June of 1969 through the efforts of Gary Winkel and Phil Thiel. Sage Publications were and are the publishers. In Winkel's introduction to the first issue he said, "A key element in the process of evaluating manuscripts . . . will be the extent to which the research rests upon empirical foundations.", followed by the phrase," . . . it is not our intention to publish articles simply on the basis of novelty of approach, intensity of verbal pyrotechnics, or weight of the author's personal authority." There is no room in this journal, then, for the sort of statements that are not empirically verifiable, but which may (or may not) be held to be *à priori* true, such as "There are no unicorns" or the axioms of mathematics. One wonders, then, how under "AIM AND SCOPE" they could solicit articles such as "studies of planning, policy, or political action aimed at controlling environment or behavior." One wonders at what sort of empirically verifiable statements would be in such articles. By Volume 14, Number 2 of March 1982, *E&B* was edited by Robert Betchtel and William Ittelson, both of the University of Arizona, with eleven Associate Editors, four International Associate Editors, and an Editorial Review Board of over forty people. Also, with that issue, it had become the official organ for EDRA, the Environmental Design Research Association.

EDRA was formed in 1968 at MIT after the first DMG international conference by Moore, Henry Sanoff, Chris Jones, L. Bruce Archer and others. Their first conference was held at the University of North Carolina at Chapel Hill in June of 1969 in conjunction with meetings of the DMG and MES (Man-Environment Systems). Sanoff and Sidney Cohn were the Chairmen and the Co-Editors of *EDRA 1,* the collected papers that have followed that year's meeting and every meeting since. In their "Preface" Sanoff and Cohn wrote:

> "The sciences, in attempting to cope [with the loss of communication between increasingly specialized tributaries] have evolved the concept of a general systems theory whereby a specialist who . . . works with a growth concept, for example, may be sensitive to the contributions of other fields if he is aware of the many similarities of the growth process in widely different empirical fields. The indicators of such interdisciplinary movement are the development of hybrid disciplines such as social psychology . . . and more recently cybernetics which grew out of electrical engineering, neurophysiology, physics, biology and economics *(sic),* information theory, management science. A simliar development is presently taking place in the field of environmental design. Faced with increasingly complex environmental problems which defied satisfactory solution, a few designers came to realize that both their traditional

problem-solving methodology and their knowledge of the man-environment system was highly inadequate ... Fortunately, however, they found a few scientists interested in studying this problem area."

The 1982 EDRA conference drew 376 people, about 30% of whom were students. You can "publish" at an EDRA conference in many different ways (including putting up a poster), since publishing in any form is the surest way to release university travel funds.

ASMER (The Association for the Study of Man-Environment Relations, Inc.) has been the labor of love since 1969 of Aristide Esser, a Holland-educated medical doctor and psychiatrist. First and foremost ASMER has continuously published *M-ES (Man-Environment Systems)*, "a bi-monthly looseleaf synergetic network for communications bearing on the interface between research in the behavioral and social sciences and the design and management of the socio-physical environment." *M-ES* now has sixteen Regional Editors around the world as well as five Subject Editors. ASMER also published monographs and directories and occasionally sponsors projects and conferences. It is an affiliate of the American Association for the Advancement of Science. The attitudinal differences between ASMER and EDRA are not great but,

> "ASMER accentuates a systems theoretical approach and orientation toward health and well-being, especially in small-scale and interior design. Furthermore, ASMER pursues information access by promoting relationships with other (non-design) organizations and consistently maintaining an international orientation."

ASMER has about 1,800 members, EDRA about 1,400. These include libraries and other institutional members. Also, there is substantial overlap in membership.

The *Journal of Architectural Research* had started in England at the turn of the decade as *Architecture Research and Teaching*. In 1974 it changed to the *JAR* and became a US-UK production with editors on both sides of the Atlantic and 300 subscribers (mostly libraries) world-wide. After several years of desuetude it is now being resurrected by University of Texas/Arlington's Andrew Sidel, to be published under yet a new name, the *Journal of Architectural and Planning Research*. In Europe, biannual conferences since 1970 have resulted in the 1981 founding of the International Association for the Study of People and their Physical Surroundings (IAPS) and the publication of the *Journal of Environmental Psychology*.

Design and environment scientists have also found berths in larger organizations. The American Psychological Association has a "Division 34" devoted to Population and Environmental Psychology, and the American Sociological Association has another unit called the Section on Environmental Psychology, which is for the sociologists. The Human Factors Society has a Section called the Environmental Design Technical Interest Group.

During the last fifteen years architectural science foliated exactly as Logical Positivism did through the thirties and scientific empiricism did in the fifties. Just as Bertalanffy was a student of Schlick and Arnheim a student of Köhler, so was, for instance, Juan Pablo Bonta (*Architecture and Its Interpretation*, 1979) a student/colleague of Broadbent. Juan Pablo Bonta, Buenos Aires bred, is the U.S.'s foremost architectural semanticist/semioticist. Thus, there is an isomorphism in both diffusion and taxonomy of discipline. We now have an architectural version of everything that had flourished on the empiricist pike since 1921.

The rest of this section is concerned with five examples of the form this third wave in architecture has come to take, for better or worse. Taxonomically, I believe they are representative, although they do not have equal length queues of soldiers behind them.

David Canter's *Psychology for Architects,* 1974.

This is a book of very scientifically cast with appeals as to why science is a good and necessary thing for architecture and how architecture science is just as good as regular science. It reviews the *Gestalt* "laws" and how to conduct an interview and how mice, men, and children learn. At one point Cantor argues "that architecture always has been, in some of its aspects, a branch of psychological research. It has just not been precisely organized enough to make it fit within the rubric of science." Also, there are paragraphs such as:

"A variable of interest (the independent variable) is produced at different levels, through the introduction of change by the experimenter, and the concomitant differences found in the other variables being measured (the dependent variables) are recorded. It is precisely because the experimenter has control over the levels of the independent variable and can assign subjects to the conditions in which they occur that he can argue that any difference found in the dependent variables is caused by variations in the levels of the independent variables."

There is nothing in this book that any well-educated architect can use or implement. It is quite clear that this was not a consideration of the author. He was, canonically, publishing. Publications are what scientists produce. If it is inflected at all it is to other scientists and, perhaps especially, science students. Further, in the range of all the things that an architect must consider the set of topics treated by Professor Canter is so tiny as to be insignificant. Even within the range of psychology (architecture experience?) it forms a tiny subset. Within that subset, if a good technical writer were to ferret out the prescriptive messages Canter is proffering and put them into simple English, they would be exceedingly banal. As that begins to sink in, the book's lack of utility becomes over-shadowed by its condescension and ignorance about how architects work. One would suppose, on the contrary, that the book would be most comprehensive since Canter is not showing us the particular fruits of his own or anyone else's research but rather that of the whole field. There are many books like this one and it is not nearly the worst. They are demanded (consumed) mostly by the set of their authors, who usually have a passage something to the effect of "architecture today is in an awful state [thanks to the other two waves of empiricism] but we have come to put things right." Above and beyond sales to libraries and their own students these books do not, unsurprisingly, sell very well. Numerous grants have been given, and contracts let, over the last fifteen years to try to translate literature like this into architect-accessible English—all to no avail.

Clare Cooper's *Easter Hill Village,* 1975

This is a book too but a rather different one. It constitutes a work in a field called "post-construction research" and, because it is constantly focused on a particular piece of low-cost housing, it is much more "applied" (but not *necessarily* more practical) than Canter's book. Further, while it was essentially undemanded (M.C.P. thesis, grants from Berkeley, the Fed and Ford) it may yet become demanded. I know several architects who have read it with benefit and, without knowing the figures, suspect that it has sold many more copies than Canter's book. Further, I suspect the book would be very widely read by architects if its 337 pages could be reduced to 150 by removing the scientific custom, if it were reorganized according to architectural rather than sociological issues,* and if she would attempt to generalize somewhat from her findings.

Finally, this book has value not just because of its scientific findings (and one wonders how many are more like common sense turned up by the spade-work) but because it is a generous, human work. Perhaps in spite of herself, one cannot help getting a good glimpse of Ms. Cooper's personality through this book and it is hard not to like what one sees. She likes people, she likes architecture, and she wants to like Easter Hill Village. This is a useful book for architects but only partly because of anything that has to do with empiricism.

BOSTI

BOSTI stands for the Buffalo Organization for Social and Technological Innovation Inc., a non-profit organization initially attached to the School of Architecture and Environmental Design at SUNYAB (State University of New York at Buffalo). The school and BOSTI started in 1969; Martin Meyerson (a planner) was then the president of SUNYAB, and John Eberhard was hired as the founding Dean. Michael Brill came to SUNYAB with Eberhard from the National Bureau of Standards.

In the beginning BOSTI *was* the School and was used as an educational vehicle to teach research to the students. Eberhard was the chief of both the school *and* BOSTI. Traditional design as such got short shrift. The students were not uniformly good research assistants, however, and some wanted to learn how to do traditional design instead. Eventually it was seen that certain inefficiencies were hurting the facility and some conflicts between the dual needs of doing research as education for students and doing research as problem-solving for real clients arose. Some students found themselves more suited to learning through studying than through doing research. While some students became excellent researchers, faculty sometimes found themselves working long hours redoing or re-writing work they felt was not sufficiently responsive to client problems.

These problems, once understood, led to a "professionalization" (Brill's word) of the BOSTI facility. It got its own unique head in 1974 (Brill) and only those students with real aptitude for the work at hand. With stability BOSTI could target its efforts at what it was not only *best* at, in terms of its human capital, but also *wanted* to do the most.

In existence since 1969 (the oldest institution of its type), its funding has shifted from 90 percent public in 1976 (base: $154,870) to 69 percent private in 1981 (base: $394,290) with an average annual turnover of $134,479 and 8.3 clients. Grants as a percent of the public sector funding are only 33 percent; the rest are contracts. Grants as a percent of *all* funding are only 18 percent. Its latest project, an investigation into office environment and productivity, has taken four years and produced a 400-page proprietary document for use by its sponsors—which include a number of Fortune 500 companies. While proprietary, it is known to challenge a rather large set of commercial interior design shibboleths.

But what is interesting about BOSTI, following deSolla Price, is its shift; in

---

*The book is about sociology to the general exclusion of technical issues. The author is not interested in how the paint held up.

becoming *demanded* it now produces economically valuable goods rather than publications for the world system of scientific information. While science produces its highly exportable cathedrals and pyramids, BOSTI is producing technology. There is no surer sign, I suppose, than the fact that on 19 October 1982, BOSTI appeared on the front page of the *Wall Street Journal*. Also, there is no reason to believe that BOSTI is any less enthusiastic about what it does today than when it opened its doors in 1969. It has simply iterated to a more synergistic (the value of the sum of the parts and their network is greater than the value of the parts considered separately) relationship with society.

SOM

In *Skidmore Owings and Merrill,* 1970, Christopher Woodward argues, or rather states, that from 1952-1961 (from the Lever House to the Chase Manhattan Bank building) SOM was in its "American" period. I would argue the contrary, that it was their European, theory-driven, period. The founding members had all made Grand Tours and Louis Skidmore was a devoted Francophile. It was the same with the next generation; Gordon Bunshaft was also a grand tourer, modernist zealot and moralist. Further, the firm embraced the Second Wave of empiricism as powerfully as the First. Nathaniel Owings argued that a large reason for their success was their ability to sell good architecture in economic terms; in his phrase, "to marinate it in sound economics." Indeed, SOM had an economic model that, after costing out a project, could "back into" a land price which told the developer if he had paid too much for the property. At the same time there are some distinctions that must be noted about this period in SOM.

SOM were theory-driven modernists but were never Rationalists. Compare the non-denominational chapel at the Air Force Academy with Mies Van der Rohe's similarly functioning chapel on the IIT campus in Chicago. However "modern" the academy chapel might be in *technique,* it is still full of the social iconography of chapelness and could never be mistaken for a mechanical equipment building, as van der Rohe's chapel frequently is.

Secondly, SOM's economic marination had a twist to it that many other firms did not. While they could meet the corporate lawyers and accountants on their own ground, i.e., bean counting, they also had a subtle and persistent way of leading non-equity "agents" of owners (the latter increasingly even more faceless than stockholders) into an attitude of taking responsibility for the environmental excrescences they were jointly responsible for. I would argue this subtle process to be an integral component of what constitutes professional method: one not of flagellating the client with a foreign theory or stripping the professional relation-ship to a single function such as skip-stop elevators, cash flow, or a dress code but of coaxing the client into a posture of social responsibility.

At its extreme, failure may result in evicting the client from the premises; drawings, contract and all. I personally witnessed such an event in SOM's New York offices but know of only that one instance. In the main the sense of care can be catching and the corporate culture has long since learned that going to SOM is a bit like going to church; it is more efficient to assume the mien of caring for your soul—and your building—before entering SOM's portals. The result of this subtle process, a process likely invisible to all known formulae for social research, is a much better corpus of work than one could reasonably expect from a firm that has long positioned itself precisely in the long-knives segment of the commercial architectural services market.

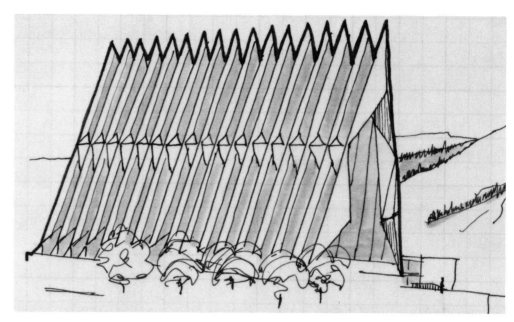

SOM Air Force Academy Chapel, 1962. There are five miles of stained glass between the tetrahedrons.

The Americanization of SOM took place, perforce and *pari passu,* during the sixties, seventies and now the eighties through a structure whose extrusions reveal a black box of uncommon managerial brilliance.

Condition number one: employees are advanced by becoming better generalists (i.e., professionals) rather than better specialists (i.e., scientists). At SOM buildings are not designed by "designers" and then forwarded to engineers to wire, heat and stiffen with a final cycle through the "spec and cost" shop. They are wrought by teams which include all these people. Thus, the engineers who do well at SOM are the ones who learn architecture, as well as *vice versa.*

Condition number two: specialties are allowed (indeed encouraged) to exist but only in a managerial grid. There are computer specialists but they are *also* architects or some other type of professional represented in another dimension on the grid. Thus, while SOM has a twenty-year history of computer applications, from project accounting to CAD (now rolling over at seven figures a year charged off equitably to overhead and projects), it is a relevant (and thus profitable) history. They are SOM, not IBM, and there's never a question about the *meaning* of this technology.

Condition number three: the order of technology and science is never confused. SOM employees write and give, on an average, as many papers and presentations as the average architecture faculty but the prior font of this firm-sponsored (and encouraged) consumption good is an investment good. In other words, new developments are professional and technical in conception and become free commodities only when they are well on the way to being amortized (used). Quoting from a report by your author, "it was made clear that the knowledge base of the professions increments through cases and that theory is dynamically induced from the frictional social context where practice takes place; rather than practice being deducted *sui generis* from theory."

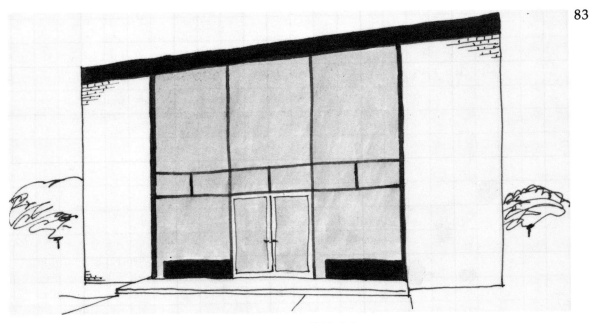

IIT Chapel, Van der Rohe, 1949–52. The sides are solid brick.

By adhering to such general professional principles SOM has permitted itself to pursue an uncommon catholicity of projects. The subtle differences in professional texture of their various offices has led them to undertake projects that vary not by building typology (houses, banks, granaries, etc.) but by a higher order of type that admits non-architectural projects. Thus, the Washington, D.C. office has taken on regional and urban policy and planning studies, the Portland office has done the well-known Environmental Study Group (1974-1979) urban-regional energy policy study (in the law section of your local library) for their home city, and the Chicago office has done pioneering work on the use of water-based heat pumps for energy conservation.

Anecdotal lore has it that when a SOM Chicago office partner was explaining the complex programming of a current hospital project to Mies van der Rohe the latter remarked, "You have to do these projects; I don't."

Inquiry by Design

This 1981 book by John Ziesel of Building Diagnostics in Cambridge is a storehouse of environment and behavior "craft" and is admirably cleansed of scientific custom. There is little in this book that shouldn't be in the portmanteau of every design student. On the other hand, if the content were cleansed just a little more and restated, it would be clear that there is little in this book that hasn't *always* been in the designer's portmanteau; often however, neglected in favor of rewarding "creativity" over responsible professionalism. Zeisel comes very close to defining environment and behavior research as a profession rather than a pseudo-science when he states:

> "If you see research methods as nothing but a set of clearly defined and highly valued rules, you can easily begin to carry out research as an end in itself—that is, as if the rules had intrinsic value."

There is an underlying pull in Zeisel's ground-breaking book toward technology (the pursuit of Value) and away from science (the pursuit of Truth), but the inertia of the home court is strong. He quotes Amos (not Anatol) Rapport ("Facts and Models" in Broadbent and Wards' 1969 *Design Methods in Architecture*):

> "Designs which are unevaluated are just assertions no matter how they are derived. Testing and evaluation are the only way of deciding whether a design is a success and of building up a *body of knowledge.*"

Zeisel then comments that "this statement could easily be adopted as the keystone for all research and design endeavors." No, it couldn't be. "Research endeavors," if you like, but not "design endeavors."

Let us examine Professor Rapoport's own "assertion" more closely. He uses a very special meaning of the word "unevaluated" to mean unevaluated by a certified E & B (environment & behavior) researcher. Is the Parthenon "unevaluated"? Is Mont St. Michel? Do the collected opinions of millions of consecutive peoples mean nothing, as in the "test of time"? Whom are we to believe when such collective opinions stretch over a thousand years and E & B research stretches over twenty? How will the results be viewed a thousand years hence should continuous culture condemn a certain built landscape and E & B research lauds it or *vice-versa*? We can be sure such cultural consenses will continue to exist. Will E & B research?

Further, Rapoport delivers a pejorative patina to "assertions." How are *his* assertions better than any architect's "assertions"? Because he postures himself as a "scientist"?

When Rapoport says that "testing and evaluation are the only way of deciding whether a design is a success" he is simply wrong. The monument to Vittorio Emmanuel II in Rome is a success and one cannot even get into it. To my knowledge E & B research has never been done on the building and even if it had it would have no effect one way or the other on the average Italian patriot. The jury is still out on whether or not "testing and evaluation" is even *one* way of determining success, let alone *the* way.

But Rapoport's fatal phrase is *body of knowledge* (source of italics unclear). In the special, scientific sense in which he uses the word there is no knowledge in the professions. There are, instead, cases. In many ways architecture proceeds like law (see Peter Collin's *Architectural Judgment,* 1971). The corpus of law is not "knowledge" in the static, scientific, Platonic sense Rapoport means. Law changes from country to country and state to state; the highest ambition of a lawyer is to change it for the better, to make it more in tune with the times. So it is with architecture. Christopher Alexander has abstracted many enduring "patterns" in the built environment but architecture as such is in continual flux—it is a river you cannot step into in the same place of twice. When I argue that Modern Movement architecture is bad I am taking a relative position, not an absolute one. Science is concerned with eternal Truth; the professions with relative value. The Movement was an over-reaction to senseless Victorian ornament and moral upheaval. As societal taste quickly drifted back to decoration as a timeless, basic, associative need the official practitioners, having passed through aesthetics into a moral and intellectual muddle from which they are still unable to extricate themselves, were left isolated from the society they were and are supposed to serve. The sustained argument in this book *against* Modern Movement architecture does not extend to resuscitation of Victorian ornament but only to a dampening of the excessive oscillation that spans *both* eras. Attempting to bail their way out through developing a pseudo-science body of knowledge will only aggravate the situation, not cure it.

Never-the-less, Zeisel's book is the most charitable work yet from a "scientist." It actually allows that the professions may have some valid methods of their own. He must be very close to the epiphany that if this charity is advanced far enough, Zeisel the scientist will vaporize into the god-head, à la Plato, and we will be left with Zeisel the designer, as actually happened in the next example.

The Conquest of Alexander

Christopher Alexander is a graduate in mathematics and architecture of Cambridge which, as we have seen, is one of the great fonts of empiricism in this century. He then went to Harvard, ostensibly to earn a Ph.D. in architecture, but in effect to write *Notes on the Synthesis of Form* (1964) and to more or less unwittingly lead the diffusion of the Third Wave of empiricism in architecture in the United States. That he quickly emerged as the guru of this movement is joint testimony to 1) the "backwardness" of the U.S. in this particular area of diffusion at the time of his arrival (timeliness); 2) Alexander's uncommon brilliance and the great success of *Notes*, which was the first thorough-going attempt to rationalize design process and integrate the new mathematics in preparation (widely supposed at the time) for electronic processing (which no one has attempted in the intervening twenty years) (enormous promise); and 3) the persistent, albeit subtle, undertone of messianic teleology that has pervaded the long rise of empiricism and fostered the convergence of science and all human endeavor vulnerable to algorithming (the perceived need for gurus to begin with).

Although Alexander has been honored with a research award by the American Institute of Architects he has never been taken up as a guru by practicing architects themselves, only by research-oriented academicians. Professions do not adopt gurus because the knowledge-procedure-process base of professions advances incrementally by cases, which tend toward anonymity, rather than theory, which tends to be identified with specific theorists. If you try to inventory the gurus of law, dentistry, engineering or medicine on one hand and attempt a similar list for religion, philosophy and science on the other, this distinction will surface quite clearly.

As was the case with Henry Ford, John Marshall, Albert Schweitzer, etc., Alexander persistently refused, sometimes rudely, the mantle of guru, knowing that progress was to be won through cases, not by others becoming like him or even by aping his theories. Thus, he progressed, as *pari passu* as SOM, from apotheosis to apostasy. After *Notes* he published four more books on design theory but each one of them was a book describing the process of fulfilling a *particular design project.* Two other books, *A Pattern Language* (1977) and *The Timeless Way of Building* (1979), are essentially one volume split into two that set out the lore required for using the "pattern language" he had developed over what must historically be the most arduous process of becoming a design professional in the history of man. These books contain the only truly useable "environmental" research yet created. Alexander's most recent work, the Linz Café in Linz, Austria, is a fine little building of extremely modest materials that will become a candlepoint in the secular, professional, humanistic tradition which includes Ictinus and Callicrates' *entasis*, the anonymous rood screens of England and

France, Saarinen the Elder's Boys' School in Michigan from the twenties and Aldo van Eyck's orphanage in Holland from the sixties.

Alexander's followers, of course, having signed on for the Way, are now left to divine It for themselves from the buildings and the books (which tell you, as they ought, how the building *in question* came about). They feel betrayed and abandoned and speak and write of their former guru in a most vituperative manner. They wanted, and expected from him, an algorithm, or set of them, that would let them become designers without the travail of essence-seeking. Alexander went as far as any person could by developing a large set of generalized patterns of historically vindicated humanistic man-environment interactions and, being able to do no more, passed through the mirror and became a designer, leaving his empiricist followers outraged on the other side.

According to the precepts of professionalism the Linz Café ought to be anonymous but cannot be because of Alexander's fame as a theorist. The people who *are* truly anonymous are the users; and just as Ford cared for no one but his customers and Schweitzer for only his patients, so Alexander in the Linz Café finally subsumed himself into a cafe patron, finally attaining for himself (and regaining for our culture) John Wood the Younger's (*A Series of Plans for Cottages . . .*, 1781) insight: ". . . no architect can form a convenient plan unless he ideally places himself in the situation of the person for whom he designs." I have no doubt that my Parisian friend who did not want Place Beaubourg in his *quartier* would welcome the Linz Café. He would come to like it more slowly and unconsciously than he came to dislike Beaubourg but ultimately the former emotion would house the greater passion.

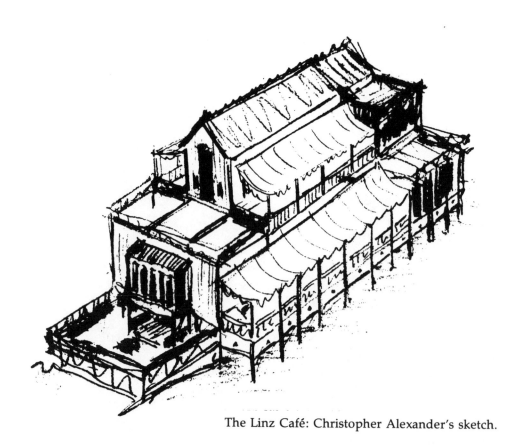

The Linz Café: Christopher Alexander's sketch.

There is no reason to believe that the production function for scientific knowledge is any different from any other production function. The inputs of money and people have exhausted their leverage. The sensitive input at this point (and at many points earlier) are scientific genius and aptitude.

Investing more money and more person power can only further corrupt, not enrich, our scientific establishment. It will induce scientists to apply themselves and their largesse where it is inappropriate as well as expensing the hidden cost of taking it from where such resources are needed. This is as true for other powerful, rich countries as for America.

At the same time that governments can do little, beyond a certain point, to bring forth scientific progress they also, beyond a certain point, can do little to suppress it. Third World countries, however, are well inside that point and since science is largely a consumption good these countries could bring forth science much better and more quickly (if that is among their goals) by investing in technology instead, which will then produce the resources to be consumed in making science.

In the meantime, in our own swamp, we have to cope with the alligators that 1) have long since flourished on expedient philosophies that provide comfortable answers in difficult times and 2) have as yet found no natural enemies.

Beware of false sciences that purport to replace rather than enrich professions. Calling oneself a scientist in order to impute a value to one's activities represents "novelty of approach, intensity of verbal pyrotechnics, or weight of the author's personal authority" to an extreme seldom found in humanistic *belles lettres*. Be mindful of T. S. Eliot's questions: "Where is the wisdom we have lost in knowledge? Where is the knowledge we have lost in information?". Computer technology was thought a science until it diffused. White-smocked scientists, gathered around their sequestered Central Processing Unit, could keep a supplicative vice-president of Union Carbide mewing for days while they considered his humble request. Now he has his own desk-top computer. What will we do with our academic departments of computer *science* when we perceive computers for what they truly are?

Yet we are not teaching nearly enough of the utility and workable, valid applications of operations research, systems analysis, computers, architecture psychology, post-construction research, etc., to our architecture and design students. What is too often taught instead is something *about* them. It is treated as theory rather than as technique. Students are enjoined to "systems thinking" or a "systems point of view." They then design, as it were, in the *style* of systems design. Or they begin to specialize as undergraduates and never design at all. Understand that the progeny of Logical Positivism are not like plague. They are not bad under any circumstances. It requires first to specify their use, limit it, and consciously exhaust the set of all possible consequences. Mindless systems-type thinking brought us systemic DDT use (for which Paul Muller won the Nobel Prize); sharp-shooting-type thinking by Rachel Carson ended its abuse. Systems-type thinking destroyed the formally rich texture of our cities; it took the sharp-shooting of Jane Jacobs, perhaps too late, to return our vision to sanity. But while not plague-like, they are closer to guns than potatoes. Unless fired a gun is harmless—but it is still much easier and more inviting to kill with a gun than with potatoes. Likewise, systems-type thinking, etc., are harmless until their full function is specified and determined—but it is also clear and consistent from its history that there is a built-in tendency to skew its assigned function, to denigrate and supplant sharpshooting, even where transparently lethal to the enterprise. Sharpshooting can include these techniques but the reverse is never true. Marshall McLuhan has shown us that the medium can affect the message but, except for television, did not much venture into how some mediums can affect messages more than others. Pacioli's double-entry bookkeeping paid for the Renaissance but did not affect its essential nature. The algorythmic universe of Logical Positivism is, in contrast, a very strong medium and can make normally conscientious and normally sharp-shooting professional men and women blind, deaf and dumb.

The difference is finally one of attitude: whether the core of our activity is Platonic-centered or Man-centered, i.e., searching for Truth and abstract Elegance instead of what benefits. Unlike the Greek architects and their preception-based *entasis*, IES engineers throughout the post-war era inflated illumination standards until the minimum for reading in 1975 was approaching the minimum for surgery in 1930, never mind the iris, the natural sun, or the cost. Apostate Le Corbusier, using his talisman *le Modulor*, a proportional human figure after Blake and Da Vinci, was the only early Rationalist architect to find his way back to a human-based architecture, a fact lost on his current revivalists. In contrast, Louis Kahn was an unrequited neo-Platonist, whose search for eternal Form has left us a legacy of mysterious, unclear and occasionally unusable buildings. The work of professionals whose cursors seek human value will always be clear to those humans for whom the value was sought; the work of those philosopher/scientists whose cursors roam on unhuman agendas, whether seeking ideal forms or the next tesserae in a scientific mosaic, will be unclear. It is the difference between order and an abstract, equipotential, and finally valueless, system. Corruption is tenable when the progeny of Logical Positivism are taught as adequate substitutes for the humanities rather than as simple tools; as a well rather than a bucket. Balconies are inevitable in Shakespeare; the cursor of design science passes over them without interest.

This sort of corruption destroys professions, from within. In "What Could Undergraduate Education Do?" *Daedalus,* Fall 1974) Carl Kaysen says,

> "What I have called the spirit of rational problem-solving is close to the spirit of science in some ways. In others, perhaps more fundamental, it is quite different. It lacks the concern with aesthetic elements of logical symmetry and generality of ideas at high levels of abstraction that characterize the deepest elements of science. Further, it is outwardly oriented, while the more fundamental part of the scientific enterprise shares with humanistic and other kinds of learning an inward orientation toward knowledge and ideas in themselves."

This "outward orientation" must never be misplaced, in any profession, or that profession will cease to exist. Architecture has come perilously close to this. Open the pages of the professionals' *Progressive Architecture* (circulation: 74,500) and compare what you see with what is inside *House and Garden* (circulation: 1 million). Do the same with the professionals' *Architectural Record* (circulation: 71,000) with *Architectural Digest* (circulation: 550,000). The contradiction not only hasn't bothered many architects hitherto; many of them took it home. Mies van der Rohe lived in a turn-of-the-century Chicago townhouse. Old friend Peg

McMillen used to tell me of Vermont skiing weekends with Walter Gropius' architecture office. She would sit slack-jawed as these zealots of all Three Waves reveled in the charm of their primitive Swiss chalet, simply not believing that she was the only one in the group who thought such hypocrisy odd.

A more practical problem is the demographic vise we will go through in the next decade. Boston University President John Silber put it very well when he pointed out that the same number of people were born in 1973 as started college in 1973. Faculties will have to contract and they will do so through retirement attrition and sacrificing non-tenured faculty, including professional adjuncts. What will be left will be those who best meet the corrupted university's new standards for promotion and tenure: those with "terminal" rather than professional degrees; those with pseudo-scientific publications rather than a professional *oeuvre*. When these people constitute nearly the whole of our academic professional role model for a generation or two, the game will be lost.

A more serious question is not what we do to ourselves but what we do to others in the community of nations. Less Developed Countries, as an unavoidable hangover from their colonial pasts, have always imitated the institutions of industrialized nations. We are living off professional fat (cultural capital) and have been for years. The LDCs have no such fat. They imitate us so that they too can be rich industrial nations, not realizing that what made us rich happened and ended in the century 1860 to 1960. Having neither fat, margin nor safety net, as it were, they are doomed if they take the same roads we have, and in a much shorter distance.

There is yet, however, room for optimism. Adolf Loos is now being studied again with suspicious curiosity. Dada, the only early twentieth-century movement that was *anti*-Logical Positivism, is regrouping. Lawyer Robert McNulty's Partners for Liveable Places, a Washington based non-profit organization that lobbies for a reasonable amount of social satisfaction in our built-environment, has sprang up and found a strong constituency, as has New York's Project for Public Places. Acorn Structures, one of the oldest running retailers of pre-cut homes in the U.S.A., has just shifted its product line to include cupolas, widow walks, dormers and bay windows—even though its *New Yorker* ads are still laid on grid paper. The *National Trust for Historic Preservation* is doing a land office business that can't be written off as mere antiquarianism. The MIT Press is now publishing a new journal, edited by Venice's Gian Carlo de Carlo and MIT's Julian Beinart whose title *Space and Society*, echoes J. B. Jackson's 1966 University of Massachusetts lecture:

> "... the study of the political aspects of the landscape should have priority. For this is how environmental design can take its place among the humanities: not by the diligent use of computers, not by the concentrating on aesthetics. The primary task is to design environments where it will be possible for men to lead the lives of free and responsible citizens, where they can give expression to the social or political side of their nature."

90

Our long trip has taken us down some wandering lanes. We always knew science was wonderful, and it still is. We now know it has two serious problems, however. The first is that it pays back so uncertainly and slowly and has so little proprietarity that it must, in the main, be considered a consumption good rather than an investment good: the money is spent for the immediate pleasure it brings. Leaders who are lead to believe otherwise find themselves forced to also believe that the dearth of valuable results simply means they haven't invested enough yet. So they spend more. And more. The second problem is that its wonderfulness easily induces pseudo-science; indeed, so easily that one suspects the tendency to be immanent. We have casually noted incursions into many unlikely fields—serious subjects for further study—and looked quite closely at the three waves that have inundated the field of architecture in this century.

Now let's look at another way of looking; a way that is at once more ordinary but is capable of transcending ordinariness. Suppose we are hurtling down a highway in an automobile and see two phenomena: a bull snoozing under an ancient oak 1000 feet away from the road—and a Mack truck which has just crossed the yellow line and is coming head on towards us. Common sense says the truck is more important. The positivist/scientific sense says they are equal in value. Now let's remove the danger and get the truck back into its own lane (no change in value to the positivist/scientist) and concentrate very, very hard on either one or the other for a period of time. Say the bull. Stop and walk to it, noting the dampness of its warm breath, its palpable body heat, the spicy but not unpleasant smell of its herbacious droppings, the flies about its face, its long eyelashes . . . Now imagine the change in your sensations if this were to be your very own bull that you had raised from its birth and had won blue ribbons with at the fair!

This new way of looking presumes that there is enormous potential *significance in almost everything and that, in varying proportion, some of the significance is inherent and some of it is projected onto it—by you, or me, or a group, or a whole nation. We can call this way of looking essence-seeking or, for the sharpshooter, looking for the bull's eye. We can also call it phenomenology. One attraction of phenomenology is the lack of specific requirements and credentials to enter the lists; no systems, no algorithms, no particular methodology. However, while it may be easy to play it is hard to play well: to develop the sensitivity and honesty to directly and authentically experience, to be able to communicate experience to others, and (hardest of all) to cause that experience to resonate with what others experience.*

The phenomenologist of architecture best known to American architects is ironically Gaston Bachelard (d. 1962), a French postman cum professor who was awarded the Grand Prix National des Lettres the year before his death. His only work in English is the Poetrics of Space (La Poétique de l'Espace) *of 1958. The best known phenomenologist of American* belles-lettres *who seriously concerns himself with the built-environment is certainly John Brinkerhoff Jackson (Landscapes, Ed. E. Zube, 1975), who absorbed well French sensibilities to geography and built-landscape during his Swiss high school years and subsequent service in Army Intelligence in the European theater.*

The competition thereafter includes Yi-Fu Tuan (Topophilia, 1974) and Robert Harbison (Eccentric Spaces, 1977). There are other souls who read, quote and write about these writers but who are hors concours *from the list itself, having elected to posture themselves as environmental scientists, which permits them to comment on everyone's environmental experience except their own—the only one that counts.**

To demonstrate this way of looking and experience we will take one minor architectural fixture, one among a large finite number of such items, and see what we can find.

*See Addenda III to this Chapter.

CHAPTER III
Towers

Et la tour de notre âme est-elle a jamais rasée? Sommes-nous pour toujours, suivant l'hémistiche fameux, "des êtres à la tour abolie"?

Gaston Bachelard
La Poétique de l'Espace, 1958

HANS

In 1969, as a guest at someone else's family reunion, I found myself with an old man named Hans. He was building a house, it seemed, and had been since 1948. When one is an architecture student one develops a perverse sense of professionalism and I recall saying to myself, "What on earth can this old man know about architecture?". By 1974 I felt I wanted to see Hans again. He had been on my mind. I wrote him, he said come, and I went by train, bus and foot, to his hermitage in rural New Jersey. I found his story an interesting one.

He was born in 1905 in a small town in northern Germany. The family was huge. There was little food in Germany after World War I, and the joy of Christmas was getting a baked apple, his only fruit for the year. His father was an upholsterer and so is Hans. In the fall of 1928 he borrowed $112 to come to America. He washed dishes in New York until 1934 when he simultaneously became a citizen and got a job upholstering. He was drafted in 1941 and spent the duration questioning German prisoners of war (and detained American Germans) in a Texas POW camp. Afterwards he visited friends in New Jersey for a while and on a long solitary walk he saw a sign offering a piece of land for sale. The price was $800, his life-savings, and he bought it that day. The next day he moved onto the site and for the next four years lived in a tent until the first habitable part of his house was finished.

The following concerns the Tower section of the house and is taken from a four-hour tape-recorded interview with Hans.

"Why did you decide to build the Tower?"

"Why, isn't it a beautiful thing?"

"Why did you build it?"

"Something round, and a round roof!"

"It really is beautiful, Hans."

Entrance tower to Hvïttrask,
Eliel Saarinen's house, 1904.

Han's tower and winding stair.

"When I say I am to build a tower everybody went crazy and said, 'What did you want with a tower?' 'What about cinderblocks?' 'Well,' I say, 'I'm going to bend them.' It was very simple. With a twelve-foot diameter the curve appears like magic. And this is the nicety of . . ."

"I'm curious about this because Jung, the psychiatrist, built himself a house near Zurich when he was about fifty. And the house is made out of two towers and the house is stretched between. He said he got strength from them."

"I don't know about that. I haven't so much strength anymore, but I would love to build . . ."

"Another Tower?"

"Yes, and to make it the real entrance to the house, right? And always my house is filled with Mozart, right?"

Jung's house, Bollingen, 1923.

Thoor, Ballylee–Yeat's house.

Since that conversation I've wondered a great deal about Towers. Jung says, in his autobiography:

"Gradually I was able to put my fantasies and the contents of my unconscious on a solid footing. Words and paper, however, did not seem really enough; something more was needed. I had to achieve a kind of representation of my innermost thoughts and of the knowledge I had acquired. Or, to put it another way, I had to make confession of faith in stone. That was the beginning of the Tower, the house which I built for myself at Bollingen ... The feeling of repose and renewal that I had in this Tower was intense from the start. It represented for me the maternal hearth ... There I live in my second personality and see life in the round, as something forever coming into being and passing on."

Jung was forty-eight when he started work on the Tower; Hans' was begun in 1952, when he was forty-seven.

One of Jung's great contributions was the "discovery" and explication of the "collective unconscious," as vast sea of archetypes: symbols, images, talismans that we all share in—whether we choose to or not. Another "discoverer" of the collective unconscious was William Butler Yeats, who says in his autobiography:

"Seeing that a vision could divide itself in divers complementary portions, might not the thought of philosopher or poet or mathematician depend at every moment of its progress upon some complementary thought in minds perhaps at a great distance? Is there nationwide multiform reverie, every mind passing through a stream of suggestion, and all streams acting and reacting upon one another no matter how distant the minds, how dumb the lips?"

Yeats was also powerfully interested in Towers. He bought a ruined tower called "Thoor" at Ballylee, in Ireland, for thirty-five pounds in June of 1917 when he was fifty-two. He got the little tower cheaply (it was part of the larger Gregory estate) because the Chief Inspector for the "Congested Districts Board" said that its value as a residence was "sentimental and therefore problematical." Yeats made an American lecture tour in 1920 to raise money for the renovation.

What did the Tower mean for him? The tie of the collective unconscious might lead a capricious mind to think of antennae, but Yeats also says:

"From the moment when these speculations became vivid, I had created for myself an intellectual solitude, most arguments that could influence action had lost something of their meaning. How could I judge any scheme of education, or of social reform, when I could not measure what the different classes had contributed to that invisible commerce of reverie and of sleep; and what is luxury and what necessity when a fragment of a gold braid, or a flower in the wallpaper may be an originating impulse to revolution or to philosophy? I began to feel myself not only solitary but helpless."

Yeats was an only child and although solitude pained him he was used to it. Certainly it was essential for writing poems. He was a poor student because as a lonely child he had developed a rich imagination that prevented him from clearing his head enough to concentrate on studies as such.

The fact of the matter is, like all symbols, Towers meant many things to Yeats. The "ivory tower," the withdrawal, the loneliness—is certainly part of it.

Another part is buried in the third paragraph of his autobiography. Yeats recalls a melancholy memory, that of "sitting on the ground looking at a mastless toy boat . . ." But he also says, in a letter: "We are at the tower and I am writing poetry as I always do here, and as always happens, no matter how I begin, it becomes love poetry before I am finished with it."

WHAT TOWERS DO

In a more general way a tower is certainly a redoubt as the towers of Bologna and San Gimignano testify. It is an eminently defensible form. I think that is at least partly behind Hans' need too. His life had been a hard one. The act of building and occupying a tower is an act of saying "I've had it; this time you're going to have to come in after me."

The kinds of towers that do not work these ways, I think, are Simon Rodilla's Tower in Watts, California, or, for that matter, the Eiffel Tower, shot towers, silos, smokestacks, etc. True Towers have to be *habitable*. Also a Tower cannot be a nuclear power station cooling tower or a skyscraper since the scale has to be human—and, at least figuratively, for one human. The degree to which it must be detached or free-standing is not clear (the examples shown are all "attached" but the Tower clearly dominates in all cases). Nineteenth century "Italianate" domestic architecture often featured corner towers, but they were seldom much higher than the rest of the house. H. H. Richardson tended to autoanthropomorphic roundness (he was fat) in his houses but the forms never quite became Towers, independent of the fabric of the wall. Carcassone is a veritable penitentiary of potential Towers but they are for the most part as imprisoned as Richardson's, stuck forever in the city wall. A good example of a 'free' embedded Tower is the entrance to Hvïttrask, Eliel Saarinen's house and studio of 1904 near Helsinki.

A Tower is, finally, a place; focused as only round (or round-like) things can be. Yeats remarks, "I was always discovering places where I would like to spend my whole life." The Tower proved quite useful in Yeats' poetry. It is, for instance the pursuit of wisdom:

> *. . . that shadow is the tower.*
> *And the light proves that he is reading still.*
> *He has found, after the manner of his kind,*
> *mere images; chosen this place to live in*
> *because, it may be, of the candle-light . . .*
> *an image of mysterious wisdom won*
> *by toil; and now he seeks in book or*
> *manuscript what he shall never find.*

Yeats also knew, through his critical faculties (which were immense), that Towers had figured prominently in the minds of other poets, other thinkers, and he specifically mentions Milton, Shelley, Villiers de I'Isle, Adam, Maeterlink, and the rather obscure Edwin Ellis who left us this couplet in 1919:

> *Mother of the hills, forgive our towers,*
> *Mother of the clouds, forgive our dreams.*

The fascination carries long distances and endures over long periods of time. Almost a century later the poet Sylvia Plath visited the Tower at Ballylee and wrote to a friend that she thought it "the most beautiful place in the world." That fall she found a house where Yeats had briefly lived near Primrose Hill in London. She was, in fact, house hunting. She was the first to apply and signed a five-year lease for much more than she could afford, elated not just because she had found a flat, but because the place and its associations seemed preordained.

By the time Yeats had won the Nobel Prize he had used the Tower as a symbol for himself, conquering the trauma of the mastless toy boat: "I declare this tower is my symbol; I declare this winding, gyring, spiring treadmill of a stair is my ancestral stair. When brings up a fascinating sidelight: The series of poems that follow "The Tower" series is called "The Winding Stair" and consists of poems about women. The winding stair is clearly the other side of the coin. In Thoor, the winding stair is inside the Tower, as at Hvïttrask and Bollingen:

> *Now that we're almost settled in our house I'll name the friends that cannot sup with us beside a fire of turf in the ancient tower, and having talked to some late hour climb up the narrow winding stair to bed . . .*

Yeats, Jung and Saarinen were happily married men. Hans' winding stair curves up around the outside. He had never married.

There are some things in life—and in architecture—that are no less valuable because they are vague. I also believe that whatever one man felt keenly, all men must feel just a little, and having a Tower here and there in our neighborhoods (to rent by the hour?) strikes me as hedging the bet.

A safer conclusion is that the humanities, whether manifested as a real human (Hans) or a dead poet or psychiatrist, harbor useful things for architects to speculate about.

Yeats' autobiography is not self-effacing: "I think the man of letters has powers of make-believe denied . . . the architect."

James Joyce's stately plump Buck Mulligan's Martello Tower at Monkstown. The Irish architect Michael Scott bought it but never lived in it, preferring to build a house next door. From a picture taken by William Armstrong.

I. The first is a passage from *The Poetics of Space,* edited as shown, and re-brought to my attention by a kind student whom I forced to read the book while I had not for fifteen years. Totally forgotten, it is none-the-less unlikely that I would have started this hen-scratching had I not once read it:

"The cosmic daydream in this passage of Bosco's book (Henri Bosco, *l'Antiquaire;* Ed.) gives the reader a sense of restfulness, in that it invites him to participate in the repose to be derived from all deep oneiric experience. Here the story remains in a suspended time that is favorable to more profound psychological treatment. Now the account of real events may be resumed; it has received its provision of 'cosmicity' and daydream. And so, beyond the underground water, Bosco's cellar recovers its stairways. After this poetic pause, description can begin again to unreel its itinerary. 'A very narrow, steep stairway, which spiraled as it went higher, had been carved in the rock. I started up it.' By means of this gimlet, the dreamer succeeds in getting out of the depths of the earth and begins his adventures in the heights. In fact, at the very end of countless tortuous, narrow passages, the reader emerges into a tower. This is the ideal tower that haunts all dreamers of old houses: it is 'perfectly round' and there is 'brief light' from 'a narrow window.' It also has a vaulted ceiling, which is a great principle of the dream of intimacy. For it constantly reflects intimacy at its center. No one will be surprised to learn that the tower room is the abode of a gentle young girl and that she is haunted by memories of an ardent ancestress. The round, vaulted room stands high and alone, keeping watch over the past in the same way that it dominates space . . .

Finally, the house Bosco describes stretches from earth to sky. It possesses the verticality of the tower rising from the most earthly, watery depths, to the abode of a soul that believes in heaven. Such a house, constructed by a writer, illustrates the verticality of the human being. It is also oneirically complete, in that it dramatizes the two poles of house dreams. It makes a gift of a tower to those who have perhaps never even seen a dove-cote. But we still have books, and they give our day-dreams countless dwelling places. Is there one among us who has not spent romantic moments in the tower of a book he has read? These moments come back to us. Daydreaming needs them. For on the keyboard of the vast literature devoted to the function of inhabiting, the tower sounds a note of immense dreams. How many times, since reading *L'Antiquaire,* have I gone to live in Henri Bosco's tower!"

II. The second is from a kind letter, written in September of 1976 after having read an earlier version of "On Towers," from Patrick Quinn:

Dear David,
       I wonder why you left out the key connection in "Phases of the Moon". . . .

>   . . .*the candle light*
> *from the far tower where Milton's Platonist*
> *Sat late, or Shelley's visionary prince:*
> *The lonely light that Samuel Palmer engraved,*
> *an image of mysterious wisdom . . .*

which suggests a more precise idea of Yeats' notion of "that invisible commerce . . ." or the collective unconscious.
      There are all sorts of strange ideas he has about negative and positive ideas and images spiralling up and down, (gyring?) like staircases

in a tower of the mind and the experience. At least it seems so in "A Vision."

I only write to you when you trigger something that comes sidling out of the depths of memory or dreams. When I was seven or thereabouts, my father took me walking (for a ramble, he called it always) in Rathfarnham. There was a strange edifice called the Bottle Tower, and nearby, the Little Bottle Tower. Two small buildings linked then by cottages and cowsheds, breaking a row of cottages, usually one-storey, slate-roofed and stuccoed. The tower was no longer lived in but served for cattle and storage. My first vivid image was of a large black cow trying to ascend the spiral stairs that wound around the outside.

For years afterwards my friends and I made occasional visits to the place, sneaking inside up to the battlemented top, creating all sorts of fantasies for our games. Usually we were shooed away by the irate cattle owner (he probably had no more than five or six beasts). The curious thing, however, is that it was most satisfying when one was alone and sneaked up without noise or notice. Then you could stay for hours. And it was a great place to daydream.

By the way, 'thoor' is a phonetic pronunciation of 'tur', the Gaelic word for tower, and it is odd that Yeats never seems to mention any local name. Most towers have local nicknames or labels, originating from early ownership or legend. His tower (Ballylee) is typical of the kind of keep; really a country house of about four storeys built by absentee British landlords for their stewards and often imitated by local mini-gentry in rural Ireland in the 17th and 18th centuries.

Another sneaking thought: Stephen Dedalus and Buck Mulligan lived in the Martello Tower at Monkstown, and Stephen talked a little about the water held in the ring of Bay and skyline. He had held up the shaving bowl of lathery water *Introibo ad altare Dei"* . . . and had reflected on the bowl of white china, full of bile, that lay beside his mother's deathbed; and, when the Bay was clouded, saw it as a bowl of bitter waters. Reminds one, doesn't it, a little of Chuck Moore's reference to a Japanese window (circular) over a wash basin, looking toward the sea, in "Toward Making Places."

It should not surprise you that my first employer, the architect Michael Scott, built his house almost beside Dedalus' tower, bought the tower, but never lived in it. Your last sentence from Yeats about the powers of make-believe denied to the architect seems supported by Michael's attitude to the tower.

Another tower that triggered my imagination about places for dreaming is probably well known to you: the wonderful aerie on the beautiful Boudrow house on Oxford Street in Berkeley, just about a half-mile north of the campus. Even my children used to say that we ought to buy the house, just to have "that neat place to go up into."

You see what you did with your wraithlike dancing among the thoughts of towers (I suspect that you had that kind of intention). You made me think too of Stevens again:

> *The stars are washing up from Ireland*
> *And through and over the puddles of Swatara*
> *And Schuykill. The sound of him*
> *Comes from a great distance and is heard*
> and
> *The whole habit of the mind is changed by them*
> *These Gaeled and fitful-fangled darknesses*
> *Made suddenly luminous, themselves a change,*
> *An east in their compelling westwardness* . . .

> Yours,
> Pat Quinn, Rensselaer Polytechnic Institute

III. Having written Chapter II over a year's period of time and having written Chapter III some years earlier I find this statement of mine, the asterisked one, curious. It raises, especially, questions regarding architecture criticism. In between I have read Juan Pablo Bona's *Architecture and Its Presentation*, 1979, and other books on this subject. Bonta's book opens with several quotes from critics, all speaking of the same building, to the various effects of "This building is ugly," "This building is beautiful," "This building is haptic," etc. Oddly enough, this is also how David Cantor's book opens (*Psychology for Architects*, 1974). Professor Bonta then issues a statement to the effect that something is very fishy here and wages, for the rest of the book, a "fight for clarity", to use Ernest Nagel's manifesto title. Clearly, Professor Bonta's remark is meant as a meta-statement, one *about* all the others. My own view is that I don't care for meta-physical statements any more than say, Otto Neurath might, but I also find them neither meaningless nor necessarily right or wrong, depending. What I find them is *removed*.

My architectural experience is very important to me or I wouldn't have spent so many years at it or have written this book. Another favorite book of mine, and not *just* because of the title is Steen Eiler Rasmussen's *Experiencing Architecture*. Never-the-less, the set of my own architecture experiences is the most important to me. Next in importance, after the set of my architecture experiences comes architecture itself. The set of architecture is important but *only* because it dependently shares (with myself) the power for generating a large subset (some I make up or dream) of my architecture experiences. The set of architecture is also much more expensive, geographically inaccessible and durable than my small, but precious set of experiences.

Third down the line are other peoples' architecture experiences. These have been, from time to time, important to me but very seldom have included any of the separate, distinct set of architecture criticisms.

Fourth down the line then are *most* of the utterances of architecture critics, which are for the most part imperative-type predications about buildings that constitute architecture experiences that *I* ought to have, or have had, or could have under certain circumstances. Now I *do* value other peoples' architecture experiences but my complaint about most, virtually all, architecture criticism is that I never learn from reading it what the authors' architecture experiences were. Instead I learn what mine ought to be, or were, or are; which I find irritating and presumptious.

The fifth set then is the set of statements about architecture criticisms (like those I just made) and I'm sure that most people, like myself, find them *removed*. It is like the difference between the pebbly, cold sting of catching a bullet pass and feeling the ground pound away under you as you run for a goal—and watching a videotape of a man watching a football game on television.

But, one asks, is not the discussion really enjoined about *Truth*? Yes, but truth about what? Who *cares* about architecture criticism? Well, I do, for the moment, because it is an excuse, however, feeble, to bring up Gilbert Ryle (*The Concept of Mind*, 1949).

Gilbert Ryle only enters Chapter II once, where it is said that he accompanied A. J. Ayer to one of the Positivist Congresses, which he did. I find it interesting that almost fifty years later A. J. Ayer still cannot figure out what makes his colleague over at Oxford tick. He admits that in his new book mentioned earlier, *Philosophy in the Twentieth Century*, 1982. The reason why is that Ryle is a problem-solver (or seeker, if you follow Peña) and that problem-solvers are much harder to categorize than system builders. Individuals (and history) have a harder time remembering them too as solved problems are less memorable than grand systems, right or wrong. Socrates, Santayana, Spinoza and Ryle were all problem-solvers but, except for Socrates' murder, who remembers them compared to great system builders such as Plato (wrong), Aristotle (wrong), Leibnitz (wrong), Hegel (wrong), or Marx (wrong)?

Ryle wrestled with Logical Positivism (a system) and its progeny in the field of psychology, Behaviorism (another system). Ryle thinks Behaviorism is great but I've always suspected that the citation of his prime example, i.e., the novels of Jane Austen, have caused some discomfort in Skinnerian circles. Until they grimace, however, we'll never know for sure. Here's Ryle:

> "The properties which we ascertain by observation, or not without observation, to characterize the common objects of anyone's observation cannot be significantly ascribed to or denied of, sensations [read 'architecture experiences']. Sensations do not have sizes, shapes, positions, temperatures, colors, or smells. In the sense in which there is always an answer to the question, 'Where is . . . the robin?', there is no answer to the question, 'Where is your glimpse of the robin?' . . . So in the muddled sense of the 'world' in which people say that 'the outside world' or 'the public world' contains robins and cheeses, the locations and connections of which in that world can be found out, there is not another world, or set of worlds, in which the locations and connections of sensations can be found out; nor does the reputed problem exist of finding out what are the connections between the occupants of the public world and those of any such private worlds."

Finally, while the Logical Positivists vainly labored for a half century over the problem of verifying humans' predications about the 'world' or 'the outside world' Ryle was having a grand time with those sets of things, equal in number to the set of sentient beings, consisting of our own private sensations. The wonderful thing about them is that while we never know if each other's predications about our sensations are lies or not we all know for a dead, cold fact that our *own* experience is true, thereby giving new vitality to the phrase 'I don't know much about art but I know what I like'. Whoever says that, the latter part, cannot be wrong at the time. Indeed, calling them wrong (i.e., lying) has been shown to abet psychosis (R. D. Laing, et al.).

Therefore, I suggest an Amendment to the Constitution requiring all architecture critics to be limited to statements in the models of:

'I think X is beautiful, etc.'; or,

'X makes me feel warm all over, or alienated, or Post-Industrial, etc.';

and shall be enjoined against statements in the models of:

'X is beautiful, etc.'; or,

X is warming, or alienating, or Post-Industrial, etc.';

Such a law would still not prevent critics from being wrong (saying false statements) because they could lie about their feelings; but 1) I believe they would be *less likely* to be wrong this way, and 2) we'll have the satisfaction of knowing they know they're lying if they are wrong. The best critics, that is the ones paid the most money, will be those that over the long run have the most constant conjunction with their readers' architecture experiences.

IV. I continue to find items. I thank Suzanne Crowhurst Lennard (*Explorations in the Meaning of Architecture,* 1979) for learning of Robinson Jeffers' boldly rusticated granite "Hawk Tower" in Carmel, California. In "The Old Stonemason" Jeffers writes:

> Stones that rolled in the sea for a thousand years
> Have climbed the cliff and stand stiff-ranked in the house-walls;
> Hurricane may spit his lungs out they'll not be moved.
> They have become conservative; they remember the endless
> Treacheries of ever-sliding water and slimy ambushes
> Along the shore: they'll never again give themselves
> To the tides and dreams, the popular drift,
> The whirlpool progress, but stand steady on their hill . . .

Further, Washington Irving's "Sunnyside" near Tarrytown, New York has along side it a free-standing tower of two stories with a bell tower on top ". . . which has no bell in it, and is about as serviceable as the feather in one's cap . . .", as he says in a letter.

SIU'S Sidney Moss has greatly increased my dim awareness that Nathaniel Hawthorne had built a tower in pointing out that Hawthorne had much admired Alexander Pope's study on top of the 70-foot tower of Stanton Hartcourt, seen while Hawthorne was U.S. consul in Liverpool. On returning to Concord in 1860, at age 56, Hawthorne began making substantial alterations to his "Wayside" (purchased from the Alcotts, who had called it "Hillside"). Chief among these alterations was the addition of a tower.

Hans was what the French call a **bricoleur**, *a putterer, a handyman—but one who was able to be quite explicit and, I suppose the best word is* **rich**, *about what it was that would crystalize his built meaning for him. We are not surprised that poets are good at that too since all they need do is change their medium. The poet Valéry somewhere puts words into the mouth of Socrates to the effect that if he were to be reincarnated he would come back as an architect since while philosophers make abstract comments about the concrete, architects must make concrete statements about the abstract.*

*But it's one thing to undertake such crystallization for one's self and quite another to do it for other people—people one knows, people one doesn't, people yet unborn, people of foreign tongues. That is the real work of the architect, not saving a few bucks on elevators or figuring out the latest wind brace gizmo. In the next chapter we will see how the profession grapples (or refuses to grapple) with this central mission. We will also study the work of at least one architect who so struggled and emerged victorious for a time. His secret was so simple it seems ludicrous: he believed architecture was connected to the rest of human life. Thus he pursued it on behalf of that human life. Henri Bergson points to this connectedness when he observed that dropping a needle has an affect on the orbit of Saturn. Marguerite Yourcenar (*Hardrian's Memoirs*, 1954), in having Hadrian describe his life-long legal counselor, Neratius Priscus, identifies this ideal professional:*

> *"His was that rare type of mind which, though master of a subject, and seeing it, as it were, from within (from a point of view inaccessible to the uninitiated), nevertheless retains a sense of its merely relative value in the general order of things, and measures it in human terms."*

CHAPTER IV
Being Between Dogma

The public understands our language, too
if we speak directly, and if there is logic
in our thoughts and if there is truth in
our words. We don't need to educate the
public. Our [architecture] has to do it.

Eliel Saarinen
Address to the AIA, 1931

During the seventies I had the fortune to make several business trips to Cranbrook Academy in Bloomfield Hills, Michigan. It was a place I was immediately comfortable in but which I could not fit into any particular dogma I had been taught as an architecture student.

The Boys' School, the first part built, covers about five acres of the several hundred acre site, and was built between 1925 and 1930 or so for George Booth, a Detroit newspaper magnate. The *raison d'être* was that Americans shouldn't have to go to Europe to study art.

Eliel Saarinen was a fifty year old architect when he come to the USA in 1923 to accept the 2nd prize in the Tribune Tower building competition. "Hvïttrask," his studio-home in the countryside near Helsinki, was built by himself and members of the firm in 1902. They lived a commune-life like and were doing work on planning and architectural projects from Budapest to Egypt. The house was rather a salon and was visited by such luminaries of the time as Sibelius, Gorki, Mahler, Strindberg, Grieg, Ibsen and Mendelssohn. Hvïttrask was a romantic pile of stone but, like several of the buildings at Cranbrook, followed the plan of buildings that had pre-existed on the site. It had a tower at the entrance that was to become a *leitmotiv* in his work. Towers figure prominently in Saarinen's work, from Cranbrook through to the Minneapolis Christ Church, which represents his later total capitulation to modernist dogma and thus ultimately won him the 25-Year Award from the AIA.

Saarinen was a born place-maker and seemed to echo Yeats' (whom he met) phrase "I am forever finding places where I want to spend the rest of my life." In transient places like hotels, or even as a house guest, Saarinen always rearranged the furniture until he was comfortable with it. Yet Saarinen's urge to make places was confounded during this era by the raging continental indecision regarding what sort of places to make. Europe was in architectural ferment then and successive waves of new and ever more loony manifestos lapped at the backwater of Hvïttrask. He had designed the Finnish pavillion at the Paris International Exposition of 1900 in a particularly lurid Hansel & Gretel style only to nineteen years later design the Helsinki Railroad Station in an equally lurid Beaux-Arts style that some have scraped hard to describe as Finnish National Romantic. He was becoming famous but floundered in the whirlpool of decaying and emerging styles. He also had done several plates, between 1900-1905, of watercolored cottages with an *art moderne* quality to them for the *Documents d' Architecture Moderne* series, to which Voysey, Haiger, and the truly bizarre Kammerer also contributed.

The Tribune Tower competition was done without Saarinen ever having seen a skyscraper. The style was a pared-down gothic and looked for all the world like some Oxbridge carillon at monster scale. In the context of Saarinen's work up until then the submission takes on the appearance of pandering rather than confusion. The winning design was only somewhat more aggressively gothic. However, Saarinen's submission was beautifully drawn and his second-place prize was to have enormous rewards for himself—as well as for us.

After he was in Chicago for the awards ceremony, the University of Michigan Dean, Emil Lorch, invited him to teach in Ann Arbor, which ultimately brought him into contact with George Booth. Booth had already built a small primary school on the site called Brookside, with his son serving as the architect. It's a quaint recollection of Cranbrook's namesake, Booth's ancestral village in Kent.

But the Boys' School (the original Cranbrook complex) was not to be like a Kentish village at all. Nor was it to be *art moderne* or adapted gothic. Even more significantly, it was not to be like any of the other complexes at Cranbrook that Saarinen built later, like the proto-fascist Cranbrook Museum with its single axis and a cascade forced onto nearly flat ground, or the Art Deco Kingswood Girls' School. Indeed, Saarinen never built anything even remotely like the Boys' School again. After Kingswood, Saarinen was fully in the grip of orthodox modernism.

The theory that I have been forced to invent to explain away the Boys' School to myself is that it is "between dogma." "Between dogma" is the style, or rather mode, that occasionally and rarely comes to fruition when, for a brief moment and under special circumstances, there is almost no style at all. That is, it is a way of building that emerges quite naturally in the moments when the forces that promote styles either recede or all cancel each other out. It also seems to help if the architect is either physically in a backwater or otherwise out of the flow of official architecture style arbitration, or perhaps because of an unusual client relationship. It has certain hallmarks and the concept has turned out to be useful in explaining numerous other buildings that had also fallen between the cracks of my received classification system.

The opposite, "Dogma," thus refers to the more familiar styles of architecture which are generated by and for architects. These styles are understandable—that is, readable—only by other architects and their cognoscenti. During periods of prevailing dogma architecture is circularly defined: it is explained and understood only in terms of other pieces of architecture. As Stephen Kurtz (*Wasteland: Building the American Dream*, 1973) has observed, this is easy to do; resemblances are as easy to perceive as differences and given that each style has its own 'language' there are bound to be enough 'cognates' to grease the wheels of critical literature forever. Architects like the dependable structure of periods of prevailing dogma for two reasons:

1) for the mediocre architect it provides easy-to-follow rules; and

2) for the ambitious architect it provides rules to bend or even fracture. The anxiety of influence makes them swerve from their precursors, to borrow the phrase again, but not so much as to go off into uncharted territory. For the clever player it provides a settled, stable game to maneuver around in.

Most of all, it follows from these rules that recognition, and therefore rewards, come only from colleagues. The game is easier, then, when you know most of the players personally—and when the results come in within six months rather than 30 years. Since the normal, using public experiences architecture just beyond the focus of awareness, to borrow yet another phrase again, it usually takes that long for authentic social opinion to resolve itself. So during periods of dogma the feedback loop is short-circuited. The architect plays to the box, not the gallery, and the possible roads to fame are so quickly explored that there is time enough in a life to try three or four approaches until you find one that clicks—like, say, Philip Johnson. Of course, all the roads have to be circumscribed within the agreed upon, ever-evolving boundaries of the dogma.

In the welters between dogma, with all precursors either obliterated by catastrophe, exhausted and discounted by professional consensus, or finally victims of an outraged public, it is slower and rougher going to becoming famous. Since the architect can't get a consensus out of the box, he or she has nothing left to play to except the gallery. There's a third alternative of listening to inner voices, like Simon Rodilla, le Facteur Cheval, or Peter Eisenman—but somehow it never really ends up as habitable architecture. The gallery, of course, represents the non-architect, non-cognoscenti citizen-of-the-earth-type and it's not without surprise that we notice that the theory comes to claim that possibilities for at least one sort of 'people's architecture' come not from changing the ownership of the means of production or abolishing the Electoral College but from a dearth of exemplars to either imitate or swerve from. While that seems like a most pleasant prospect for society, it must be borne in mind that it carries two pieces of real terror for the architect: a substantially broadened responsibility to a much larger community and a lack of clear instructions about how to fulfill it. Saarinen spoke to this *angst* in his 1931 address to the AIA: "We do not need to educate people. Our art has to do it." In other words, if you are to play to the gallery, it has to be in terms that the gallery can understand. This gives rise to the single most salient hallmark of architecture between dogma: it is capable of being 'read' by ordinary people and its literary content consists not of references to other buildings or abstract formal concepts (which the public can't read) but to the themes, events, topics, signs and symbols that are common to everyday life. This doesn't mean "literary" in Tom Wolfe's sense that you need a book to understand it but, on the contrary, literary in the sense that you can *read* the architecture directly, without special knowledge, keys, or training.

By contrast, architecture under dogma reminds us only of concepts, ideas and images that are special and masonic to the world of professional architecture. Architecture between dogma reminds us of ourselves before we became architects: of truths, myths (comforting lies) and the daily experience that we share with all literate members of our race and nation. 'Environmental education' began to catch on in the sixties not because the public suddenly became stupid but because we had replaced the building stock over a forty-year period with artifacts that resisted reading.

Creating between dogma was easier for Saarinen at Cranbrook than for most. Detroit was as much of a backwater as Helsinki was. At Cranbrook he was a foreigner learning a new tongue. Convoluted dialectic about the subtleties of architectural movements was impossible. He was now far from the burgeoning, obsessive chatter of Vienna, Darmstadt, Paris, Weimar and the Low Countries. Also, Finland, and the Scandinavian countries in general, had never had the kind of tension between the old styles and the new that Central Europe had. The Beaux-Arts had never really taken over in those climes to begin with.

Thus at the Boys' School there was a relaxation of the requisite effort to be different, daring and individualistic found in the capitals of Europe, New York and even Philadelphia. The family worked together (his wife Loja did the tapestry and carpeting; his son Eero did the drafting) and Eliel worked closely with the craftsmen, so that serendipitous changes and additions could be made along the way. Bricks went more or less where they ought to, not where they wanted to be or where some exogenous style said they ought to go. Saarinen once said he aspired to be as smart as, and as dumb as, a plant.

In my own analysis, I look for hallmarks in the four categories of surface, symbol, movement and place. Surfaces because that's what ordinary people see and respond to. They see walls, not space. Only specialists see space. Between dogma efforts are naturally made to make use of walls as a bed for symbols, to explain how the building is organized through fenestration and to explain the walls themselves as well. That is, surfaces are crafted in such a way as to clearly show how they are made and numerous devices are introduced to reveal the materials and let you know how far away from it you are and how big it is. This is a sophisticated business and, freed of the exigencies of style, Saarinen revealed himself as a master of it.

Symbols and signs serve to explain, often quite literally, the function of the unit, the general purpose of the place, or the nature of the inhabitants. Carvings of *putti* holding scientific instruments, for instance, as a door surround, identify the observatory. The Boys' School is full of priapic imagery (as befits boys) with some orphic imagery near the edges. Kingswood, the Girls' School built in the thirties, has far more orphic imagery but it's more easily lost among the jumble of more purely decorative elements.

Movement is used not for demonstrating sculptural pyrotechnics of inter-penetrating space, line and color—a self-absorbed dance that excludes the user—but instead for the simpler, more human act of confirming and celebrating the fact that one is moving from one place to another. The key is that the centrality of the action is on the person moving, not on building materials.

Place is a more complicated concept but essentially follows the centrality mentioned above, but without the movement. Aldo Van Eyck, who has tried to struggle against dogma, said that we need "place and occasion" instead of "space and time." Saarinen had a marvelous way of nailing down place through the careful orientation of outdoor seating and contrived functions. Contrived functions are little white lies like sticking a fountain, ostensibly set up for watering horses, next to a parking lot. Aside from the delight of the moving water, it nails down the placeness by adding historical depth to the function. It also may turn out to be prescient, given the price of motor fuel.

Some other examples may help to illustrate the theory as I understand it.

All architecture before architects is understandably between, or rather before, dogma. The painted caves in the Auvergne are quite literal, as is native American Architecture. Indians all over both Americas slathered their structures with insignia of all types. Most of it was painted rather than carved so we've lost it. Egyptian, Mesopotamian, Far Eastern and even Hellenic architecture were very between dogma. Vitruvius (*The Ten Books on Architecture*, c. 75 B.C.) tells us that the caryatids (columns in the form of standing women) on the Erechtheum in Athens and the Treasury in Delphi are there to commemorate a military victory over Caryae, a state in Peloponnesus. The women are there "to appear forever after as a type of slavery, burdened with the weight of their shame and so making atonement for the State." One wonders what meaning the caryatids could possibly have at the Highpoint II Hotel in London by Berthold Lubetkin. Lubetkin's women are holding up the roof of the *porte cochère* there. Why aren't they men, perhaps in the uniform of the German V-2 Rocket Corps?

Romanesque was between dogma, especially in provinces like Bretagne, where gory, explicit stone calvaries were felt necessary to get the story across. Gothic windows and sculpture were very between dogma but a schism is already becoming apparent between the architecture *qua* architecture and the *appliqué* of communicators in late Gothic. Italian Renaissance gardens were very between dogma but not French Renaissance gardens. Revivals are almost by definition not between dogma because they're resurrected by architects as pure style. Thus they tend to lose their original literary content and retain only their formal virtues—at least partly because the revivalists often do not know how to read the literary content right in front of their faces. The sick side of revivalism is 'Camp', and Hilton Kramer ("Postmodern," September 1982, *The New Criterion*) extends critic Charles Jencks thusly: "The 'underlying genesis of Camp in architecture,' Mr. Jencks points out, lies in 'the movement of formalism'—which is to say, in an architectural aestheticism that has divorced itself from its functionalist origins and become pure style."

It goes without saying that International Style was dogma as it had never been before. Almost all WPA projects, however, built when modern architecture was just getting its steely grip on the USA, are very between dogma and quite uniform in their high quality. This is because of a special relationship between client and architects as mentioned earlier and as exemplified in this case by the Public Buildings Act of 1926 which specified "artistic enrichment through . . . imagery that expressed the governmental function of each structure."

Specific buildings to look at besides the Cranbrook Boys' School, would have to include Goodhue's Nebraska State Capitol, The Pension Building in Washington (with a frieze that recounts the entire Civil War with original cast), the Department of Labor there, Mount Hood Ski Lodge in Oregon, the Monument to Vittorio Emmanuel II in Rome, the rood screen in St. Etienne du Mont in Paris and—for a modern example—Aldo van Eyck's orphanage in Holland. Eyck used another, more aleatory, associative technique I call nature-trapping; dished out bowls in a concerete apron to fill with rain water and other little tricks to keep you mindful of the processes of nature (see illustration in Chapter VI). Most modern architects do this with leaky roofs.

The moral to the theory is that we are in a phase now where such forces (actually the absence of them) put us, in general, between dogma again (probably for as short a period of time as usual) and I'm anxiously awaiting its instance. Decoration is coming back, we see, but has so far been limited to the revivalist mode, serving only to recall other buildings or styles. The efforts in the forefront thus far have been exquisitely intelligent; we'll know we're making progress when they become intelligible as well.

Bird's eye perspective of Cranbrook School by Eliel Saarinen, 1926.

Surface & Sign: Galileo Door, Observatory Tower, 1927. Geza Maroti, sculptor.

Symbol: Cranbrook School rams' head carving—one of the more subtle allusions to the fact that this is a boys' school.

Movement: main gate to Cranbrook School, 1925–30.

Place: Cranbrook School Quadrangle.

110

It is not true that the tension of dogma does not affect "ordinary" people, meaning non-designers. In periods when a dogma is in full-cry it greatly reduces peoples' options. In periods of lousy dogma, such as the modern movement, it consistently dishes out lousy architecture. What can you expect when architects design for each other rather than . . . people?

Ordinary people are the subject of the next chapter, one written with a somewhat lighter-hearted tone that belies the seriousness of the subject. Ordinary people are serious business for several reasons but the most important is assiduously avoided; namely that these are the folks who pony up the money. Without ordinary people architects get to not only build for each other but also feed each other.

Francis Ventre, writing in the December 1982 issue of Progressive Architecture, *produces figures that show that many of these folks are getting tired of ponying up the money. And why not? If architects produce buildings that feel like they were designed by an engineer why not just hire an engineer?*

CHAPTER V
Ordinary People

The architect is a sort of theatrical producer, the man who plans the setting for our lives. But this producer job is difficult for several reasons. First of all, the actors are quite ordinary people.

Steen Eiler Rasmussen
Experiencing Architecture, 1959

By people, I mean all those not routinely exposed to architecture education and practice and who live around here, in industrial or, if you wish, post-industrial societies. These people are in buildings far more often than not. They are born in rooms and die in rooms. They are occasionally fatally wounded outside but are always brought in to expire. Architects may be the designers, but all those people are the design-processors. As processors they design as well as they can. At the scale of the home appliance they can design a lot by deciding which to buy. At the level of architecture they are limited to opening or closing their eyes. Occasionally, but not often, the more well-to-do of these people are clients or serve on a committee or board that is a client. It is a lot like jury duty. It is vaguely uncomfortable from the start, something you are statistically not likely to do and are surprised by. When it happens, you bear with it because the odds of your doing it again are infinitesimal. But it's also exciting, in a way, because suddenly you are a form-giver, a place-maker, and although the architects know much more about damp-coursing than you, you easily know just as much about design. If your doctor or lawyer tells you what to do, *you do it.* Everything your architect says you regard with suspicion because 1) you intuitively know there's more than one "right" way to do much of it and 2) while you haven't hung around a lot of operating rooms or courts you certainly have seen a lot of buildings and even more in pictures.

However, there are two differences here. One is that the architect has some unusual mental equipment you might not know about and the other is that although you have *looked* at many buildings and pictures of buildings you have probably really *seen* very few. After many years at this, I still do not feel I have really *seen* a building until I have drawn it. And while you have been in many buildings you have probably *self-consciously* experienced few, if any. People are notoriously bad witnesses, often missing blatant features or not remembering the colors only seconds later. We may have the same business on our retinae but we all process it differently. The heart of architecture after all, is neither buildings nor people but the relation between the two. "Relations," as Bertrand Russell and others have pointed out, have no denotation. You can't have a pound of it, as you can of either buildings or people. The abstract quality of this is too seldom present in architects' minds and hardly ever in ordinary people's.

While most education stresses atomistic vision, analytic process and linear progress, the study of architecture must, and in the best of places has, combined these skills with the ability to quickly shift from atomic to pattern vision, synthetic process and all-at-once decision-making. Most peoples' ability to perceive at the level of patterns is limited to those times when their glasses fog up or during half-time at football games when all those little cards are held up that magically become Lincoln's profile. That's very different stuff and stands at the heart of the ability to design syncretically: to take data that in a complicated project like a spoon quickly approach infinity and yet create a concept(s) that is likely to generate suitable patterns and appropriate details. There is none of this, no attempt to inculcate, *any* of its web of skills in "normal" education. The only other places that come close in higher education are business education case courses, science dealing with morphology, higher mathematics and theoretical physics.

Also, there's the fact that the architect's inventory of buildings and places is likely to be greater and the quality of his or her *experience* of them tends to be better. One important distinction to get out of the way: architecture is meaning-less, unimportant, episodic and numbingly expensive. Architectural *experience* is full of meaning (in both the drink-as-deeply and the mere associative senses of the word), always important whether conscious or not, fluid and usually free. If there's a fee, it's usually cheaper with a student ID. Remember the quote from Robert Sommer in Chapter I? *"Most people experience the environment just outside the focus of awareness."* This means that you are not often well-connected to how either the pieces or the whole of the environment is processing you (and vice-versa) with the result that 1) it seems less important than it really is, 2) you often make diagnostic errors in trying to improve your comfort (in both the sensible and psychological senses of the word), 3) you can't really design worth a hoot (sorry), 4) you are probably a lousy client, 5) you're getting less out of life than you could otherwise, and 6) you're often irritable.

It *seems* unimportant because you are not conscious of the impingement. The gap closing—the experience becoming self-conscious—is particularly powerful because it has the quality of soup-spat-in (from an old Russian proverb to the effect that things are never quite the same again). Fortunately, it becomes increasingly easier to have these little epiphanies all by yourself once it has happened to you, usually with help. As in being able to realize that "Chock Full 'O Nuts" seats are purposely engineered to be uncomfortable after fifteen minutes, for instance. Or better yet, to realize this from the *first* minute. It becomes, after that, hard to go back to being a passive victim. I call the process of becoming aware of our experience among inanimate objects *environmental education.* It is most definitely not environmental *design* education although it probably ought to somehow precede it. Design educators assume that environmental education happens in the studio, as a by-product of learning how to design. There is no evidence to support this. The students instead learn how to emulate instead of design and how to recall instead of experience. As a consequence they often become stylists instead of designers.

Environmental education, as I have described it, usually occurs in architectural graduates for other reasons besides their formal education. An astonishing number (of those who have experienced this) can tell you where and when the epiphany occurred.

Some simple short incidents will further explain what I mean by environmental education and gap-closing. A favorite exercise in workshops on environmental education is called "spatial history." This is where everyone relaxes and closes their eyes except the leader. Then, talking softly and meaningfully he or she will begin, starting when we were babies, making up a fictive history of all the places where we have lived, slept, been, etc.; taking us into our rooms, smelling the smells, touching the cupboards and the nubbly bedspreads, remembering the sound of the light switches, the feel of the closets, etc. And then afterwards asking for the best, the worst, the most poignant or powerful, etc., experience any of us can remember. There are some interesting patterns: women remember steps, rooms, the quality of light, and the proximate outdoors; men remember halls, cellars, sounds and the nearest big field. And while people won't remember much of the monumental thing (the Empire State Building, the Smithsonian) they went to see once, they *will* vividly recall years later a bright dress they saw there or what kind of sky it was that day. Anyway, three specific anecdotes will suffice, two from Texas and one from Oregon:

When we had gotten done with the exercise and a couple of people had recited glorious experiences in detail long forgotten, our attention was suddenly taken up by the fact that a fortyish woman was crying. She did not have, it turned out, a *place* she treasured but rather an *event*. Raised in a large family on a ranch, she had never had a bedroom to herself. Every six weeks it was her turn to walk over to grandmother's house alone on Saturday morning and sit in the kitchen with her while she baked gingerbread cookies. At noon grandfather came in from the fields, the three ate lunch and she then walked back with a bag (and a tummy) full of gingerbread. She had left from there straight for the state teacher's college and a shared dorm; and from there straight into a two-bedroom rancher, with a husband for a roommate. She commuted to graduate school after having some children. She was crying, really, because she had never had a room of her own. She pulled herself together and was encouraged to draw a plan of her house on the blackboard. There was a room there often referred to as a "den." They are hardly ever used for anything. Ostensibly a "man's" place, men usually prefer a command-post scale chair with out-buildings (end tables, ottoman) at the edge of the traffic flow through or by the living room, so that they can pretend to read while waiting for someone to ask them how they are. They'll usually settle for a technical-type question. Dens are usually reserved for storing ping-pong tables with torn nets. When last we spoke, a year later, the den in question had become a "sewing room," somewhat reduced in scale by moving a wall, and was equipped with a command-post type chaise with out-buildings, no sewing machine at all, and many attractive Impressionist reproductions on the walls. The paneling was painted yellow and no one—*no one*—else was allowed in.

Another person, a man this time, spoke of how he remembered his family sitting around the fire as a child and how much he (suddenly) missed it. This seemed odd since his present house *had* a fireplace. However, since there were doors in the wall on both sides of the fireplace, even though one was at some distance away, the fireplace became a two-dimensional facade and the "place" a hall, not a hearth. So one of the doors was nailed shut. Sometimes it doesn't cost much.

The last story is of a woman who fondly remembered long periods of reading as a teenager and wished that somehow she could find time to read these days. She had the time—it was the place she was bereft of. She had a fine recollection of favorite reading places from the houses she grew up in and none anything like them now. She left full of enthusiasm for the project. I believe she was ready to tear her house down stick by stick looking for the place she didn't know she missed.

These are the kinds of things you would likely do if you were truly aware of your environment. It can make you change banks, get up in an interview and start moving the furniture around, move to another city, change jobs, etc., when you begin to realize how much it really affects you. Saarinen the Elder was reputed to rearrange the furniture in his hotel rooms. Why do your children misbehave in some restaurants but not others? Why do I like meeting friends at this corner? Why did Antonioni spray paint the park in *Blow-up* a different shade of green?

It's true that architectural experience of this sort will always, even in the best of worlds, remain a lot like jazz (little old lady: "What is jazz, Mr. Armstrong?" Armstrong: "Lady, if you don't know I can't tell you.") Certainly the efforts of the small band that do these kind of workshops aren't going to get anywhere. And the real estate section of the paper will stay the same, forever treating architecture like a stereo system, listing its *features* instead of its *value* (3 Br, 1½ Bath, Cath ceiling, etc.) And the large circulation slick magazines will continue to detail their "art" journalists to writing about architecture. Our only even *modest* hope is in some changes in K-16 education.

But at the same time as we think fondly of the time when primary school children will be nourished in such a way as to keep the process of conscious affect from the environment alive, architecture too has a responsibility to come halfway. Rather than bemoaning the fact that people *do not* react to their environment *directly* we have to also capitalize on the more indirect ways that they do. In fact, people *do* respond (as well as they can) to environmental experience as they do the multitude of other events in their lives—in a literary way. They want pictures and music explained, literally, so they can understand them. Pictures and music are obtrusive, commanding attention and, therefore, also explanation. The experience of landscape or architecture seldom comes with a frame around it or out of a speaker or instrument and seems not to need explanation. But although less obtrusive, it is far more pervasive—and therefore influential. Pictures can be avoided in a number of ways; so can most music. The experience of our environments, by definition, cannot.

On the other hand one has to speculate on the reason for the explosion of "environmental awareness" about the built-environment in the sixties. Was this now necessary because people had gotten dumber? Or because the buildings had? In other times buildings reached out to peoples' way of understanding— met them halfway—by offering them associative "handles" to access the experience. Hand-craftsmanship and decoration reminded them that people very much like themselves had something to do with the thing. Sculptures of things they were likely to see everyday—people, dogs, plants, etc.—make further ties to the way they perceived the rest of their experiences. Spatially, the rhythm of columns, the articulation of windows and bays, the clean division of stories, all seemed to relate larger areas to the scale of their own bodies. Inside these were niches, baldachinos, balconies, doorframes, chair rails, nooks and so forth to do the same. Some buildings even had rooms.

Modern architecture, as we have seen, came from new philosophies (Logical Positivism) and new psychologies (*Gestalt*) as overheard in coffee houses from Vienna to Utrecht after the turn of the century. One consequence of Modern architecture was that architecture became "unreadable" by ordinary, literary people.

It was predicted, interestingly enough, by Victor Hugo, who wrote a fascinating chapter in *The Hunchback of Notre Dame* called "This Will Kill That." It's left out of most English editions as it is totally gratuitous as regards the advancing of the plot. His point is that in societies where most of the people were illiterate, buildings served the purpose of books, and that the proliferation of books would kill architecture. Churches had large parts of the bible routinely told in carvings— all over their surfaces. The roodscreen, a large panel separating the nave from the chancel, was devised expressly for this purpose. The hagiography on the Russian Orthodox iconostases do the same. Local favorites and patron saints went on the front. Stock highlights went on the glass. It takes a full day to read the windows of Ste. Chapelle in Paris. Greek temples did battle vignettes in the gables. It continued until quite recently; I've mentioned earlier the terra cotta frieze of the Pension Building in Washington. It tells the entire story of the Civil War on all four sides. But in other places, particularly the late Beaux-Arts in France and Victorian England, the story-telling became gibberish, thereby providing some of the negative side of the *raison d' être* for the Modern Movement.

Hugo claims the culprit was printing, which would make "readable" buildings obsolete. Why read a building when you can get a paperback? His prediction was startlingly correct but I'm not so convinced of the causal dynamics. If his reasoning is right why do so many people go to see movies made from books they've just read? And although you can carry a paperback, you can't read it while you walk. People didn't stop reading buildings—architects stopped making buildings that could be read. For a number of reasons, people—the vast majority of ordinary people and even a few lonely architects* of the period—have never liked modern architecture. One could list the reasons. There are some recent books that try to. But it is *sufficient* reason to try again another way that people have been gratuitously denied a simple way of associating themselves with, and therefore feeling that they have a part in, their built-in environment. To be sure, pop-architecture keeps the tradition alive but many people, including cab-drivers, want to believe that there's more to life than a huge Jack-in-the-Box, or a 12-foot hot dog on top of a fast food stand, and could use some evidence of it.

There's one example that's so startlingly clear it must be illustrated. There is a building in Rome called the Monument to Victor Emmanuel II, designed by G. Sacconi. It is as gaudy as you can get. The equestrian statue in front is so large that a sit-down dinner for ten can transpire in the horse's belly. It has angels, eagles, bundled shafts and flights of steps galore. It is the only white building in Rome, Italy being too poor to clean the others. The building celebrates the unification of the city states of Italy, an accomplishment in which Emmanuel II played a great role.

---

*See Ralph Walker's wonderful *The Fly in the Amber,* 1957, author published.

Italy was the last European country to do this and many thought it could never be done. Every architect I've ever met who has seen this building hates it—it's garish, it's too too—everything. Every Roman I've ever met (except Roman architects) loves it. Its seams are bursting with meaning. During the recent successful Italian bid for the World Cup in soccer the immense Piazza Venezia in front of the building was full until dawn with wildly cheering Italians. They would think of going nowhere else. Something is out of joint here—the polarity is just too vivid.

How do I get off writing about "people," you might well ask. Am I not one of *them?* Yes and no. Unlike the majority of architecture students, I came to it with a degree in liberal arts. Of course, it *did* happen to me. I became "visually" oriented, lost the ability to spell, etc. But the armor of a liberal education protected the vital organs and sometime later, standing at the rear of Chartres, I passed back through the mirror and became a lay person again. I had brought all my history lecture notes, etc., to Europe looking to flesh out, one by one, my history slide lectures with the real thing. I did, and was both elated and disappointed to find that the learning experience has *almost nothing* to do with the witness experience. Architecture was suddenly much less important because I found out that the experience was enormously diluted by how I was getting on with my wife that day or how lunch was. Architecture was suddenly much more important than I had thought it was now that, out of school, I could see how strongly it influenced my relations with my wife or made lunch much better or worse. And that the functions in question seemed to be unmoved by this or that building's succession in history. Now I can move back and forth through the mirror, although I get faint if I do it more than twice a day.

Monument to King Victor Emmanuel II, Rome.

The next chapter constitutes the empiricist argument against empirical architecture and I present it, in blatant violation of Ockham's razor, because I still receive requests for copies. Imagine what's going on here: you're in college studying to be an architect and you want to put meaningful ornament in your designs but the prevailing rationalist dogma says "don't even think about parking here." Not in so many words though. There was no sign saying "no smoking or ornamenting" hanging in the studio. After all, no sign is deemed necessary to keep one from digital-nasal exploration in church.

Of course it was subjectively, intuitively, experientially self-evident to me (and several others); why have faceless, blank and finally meaningless buildings when we can have nice ones instead, like in the old books in the library? Our tiny band consisted of moles with liberal arts education of varying qualities and durations, but enough in each case to see the emperor's clothes. No wonder architecture faculties prefer matriculants straight out of high school. They can french fry their brains without so much as a chirp.

Like the proverbial rat in the maze I took the only way out: I sacked the library for every piece of empirical, scientific, pseudo-scientific evidence I could find that ornament, any ornament in architecture, was good for mental health and then I tried very hard to write it up just like they did. It was our manifesto, and a start.

CHAPTER VI
Environmental Disassociation

"Where are you from" inquired the Red Queen. "And where are you going? Look up, speak nicely, and don't twiddle your fingers all the time."

Alice attended to all the directions, and explained that she had lost her way. "I don't know what you mean by your way," said the Red Queen.

Lewis Carroll
Through the Looking Glass, 1872

A substantial amount of highly specialized research has been done on isolation, sensory deprivation and sensory overload. It was done in the fifties at McGill as a response to Korean brainwashing and the needs of the submarine service and again in the sixties by NASA for space travel. Simultaneously, much theoretical research went on at the Menninger Clinic, at Harvard and at several mental hospitals throughout the country.

The people who design the environment have the responsibility, realized or not, of controlling these functions to a substantial degree. Methodologies become a good deal messier when attention moves from the clinical laboratory to the complex fields of architecture, interiors and planning, but the necessity of such a move is obvious none-the-less.

PSYCHOLOGICAL BASES FOR DISASSOCIATION

The experimental work of the people working in sensory deprivation/overload and isolation figures centrally into this discussion. It is important to remember, however, that these people were working with extremely specific environments and were looking at the results through extremely specific lenses. The reason, of course, has to do with the difficulties of researching complex environments and gauging subjective responses. It's difficult to be "clinical" with a great many variables. Sensory deprivation is a special subset of disassociative phenomena but one that looms important simply because it's the area where the most research has been done.

Several investigators, Goldberger and Holt especially, have mentioned David Rapaport, a psychological theorist, as a touchstone for a conceptual framework upon which a great many sensory deprivation phenomena becomes explained. The same theories provide a groundwork on which to explain disassociation in general. Rapaport maintains that the ego structure and its stability is dependent for its continuity on stimulus nutriment (Piaget's phrase) from the environment—to a degree depending on the individual. Restated in another way he explains that the stimulus deprivation experiments withdraw that stimulus nutriment which, conveyed through the senses, is necessary for the maintenance and effectiveness of elementary reality orientation. The ego is always somewhere on a scale of either being autonomous with respect to the environment or being nearly totally affected by it. Rapaport mentions some conditions which might impair the ego's autonomy from the environment. Among them are lack of privacy, stimulus deprivation and loss of memory or verbal supports.

Goldberger and Holt, in testing these ideas clinically with observations and interviews of subjects exposed to isolation, have come up with the following observations:

"Working within a psychoanalytic conceptual framework, we viewed the isolation situation as one in which normal *reality contact* is subject to significant interference. By the term "reality contact" we mean perceptual contact with significant, structural aspects of the external world via the exteroceptors. . . . Thus, we were led to the theoretical formulation, which has been advanced by Rapaport, that the functions of the secondary process depend for their maintenance on continual contact with reality, and the absence of reality contact facilitates a regression to the primary process."

Following the same line of thought is the following from the work of Ruff, Levy and Thaler, contained in the same volume.

". . . the experiment separates the subject from sources of information which ordinarily make the environment meaningful. He responds by attempting to restore meaning to the situation. This is done by structuring the experiment to provide a sense of continuity with previous experience.

Each individual employs an internal frame of reference to maintain his relationship with external reality. As long as this structure remains intact, he can compensate for the loss of input from the outside world . . . Our formulation, therefore, is that isolation "destructures" the environment. The subject responds by restructuring to create a sense of continuity with his previous existence. He thus restores meaning to the situation. The experiment will be tolerable only as long as the sense of continuity is maintained.

What remains unclear is just what is it that sustains the dynamic of "reality contact" and makes the "environment meaningful?" The difficulty is trying to analyze disassociation or the breakdown of the ego structure as a specific state isolated in time. If viewed as a dynamic, a process through time, successive mental states become clearer in relation to each other. What seems to be the case is that a person's ability to cope with the "present" depends on his ability to relate his immediate experience to his past. As Kierkegaard remarks, "Life must be lived forward but understood backwards." A person's past, his whole experience, acts as a bulwark or a modifier to the present. The memory is a bank out of which an autonomic selective associating process pulls information and compares it and relates it to immediate experience. The breakdown, disassociation, occurs when no communication or when conflicting communication exists between the past and the present. It is this relationship and dependence on the past which makes the disassociative experience functional with respect to the individual. Given the same phenomenon, each person has a different set of past experiences to relate it to.

SUSCEPTIBILITY

Before stating those features of the personality that make some people more vulnerable than others it is important to point out that no one is left unaffected by the environment. Hale categorically states that "the environment should never be regarded as passive in any respect..." Maslow, in his article "Isomorphic Inter-relationships between Knower and Known," points out similarities in form that develop between the perceiver's self and the world he perceives:

> "... The more whole the person becomes, the more whole becomes the world. It is dynamic interrelation, a mutual causation.
>
> As Emerson said, 'What we are, that only can we see.' But we must now add that what we see tends in turn to make us what it is and what we are. The communication relationship between the person and the world is a dynamic one of mutual forming and lifting-lowering of each other, a process that we may call "reciprocal isomorphism." ... a higher order of environment tends to lift the level of the person, just as a lower order of environment tends to lower it. They make each other more like each other."

The general case for environmental interaction stated, it becomes increasingly difficult the more specific one gets. Ruff, writing alone, points at some of the complexities:

> "Whenever a man is placed in an environment that blocks gratification of such needs, stress may arise. Furthermore, it is not essential that gratification actually be blocked. Men respond to symbols or threats of frustration before it exists in fact—or even when there are no realistic grounds for assuming that it will exist. Any potential cause of deprivation may be looked upon as a source of danger and will elicit a response, depending on the need that is blocked and on the individual."

Interviews to discover why people react the way they do are made difficult because, as Robert Sommer says, "People are not sure what it is about a building or room that affects them, nor are they able to express how they feel in different surroundings." This is so partly because, as E. T. Hall has observed, people treat space like sex; we all know it's there but no one likes to talk about it, and partly because people have gotten used to adapting to their environments rather than changing them. The muteness of architecture and the futility of blaming inanimate objects conspire to make people adjust to rather than confront their surroundings.

Nevertheless, several investigators have tried to find out the individual differences in reacting to disassociative influences. One, the most obvious, has been mentioned before: the person's past. Everyone tends to structure his behavior according to certain expectations about the kind of events he is used to. It is as if each individual makes his environment less chaotic by organizing his experiences according to a hierarchy of probabilities. Sommers points out the fact that perception differs for natives and non-natives since their ability to make associations will differ drastically. Ruff, Levy and Thaler point out that each individual has his own frame of reference to maintain his relationship with external reality and that so long as this structure remains intact he can compensate for destructive or limited input, but when the artificial image of normal existence collapses, the subject becomes defenseless against repressed material.

People react to sensory deprivation and isolation as a function of ego strength. A person with a strong ego will not tend to be overwhelmed by primary process intrusions. When he fantasizes he is still in control and can revert to goal-oriented secondary processes whenever he wishes. He tends to enjoy the threatening situation and takes it for what it's worth. On the other hand people with weak egos cannot stand the intrusion of the primary processes because they can neither handle the intrusion nor the drives that accompany them. Fantasies, libidinous daydreams, etc., all are accompanied by guilt and anxiety. In Goldberger and Holts' words:

> "Individual differences in reaction to isolation may be accounted for . . . by assuming that people differ significantly not only in the extent of their dependence on reality contact for maintaining efficient secondary process thought, but also in their resistance to regression and in their general modes of handling the primary process once it begins to become evident in the conscious stream of thought."

Some authors have attempted to get quite specific (because they have been asked to do so by NASA or the Defense Department) about personality structures resistant to disassociation. Chambers and Fried list these characteristics: confidence, psychological stability, respect for the project at hand, not overly dependent, a person presenting appropriate and predictable reactions (yet adaptable), no inner conflicts, an ability to function where normal behavior is impossible and an ability to tolerate both extreme association and isolation.

Goldberger and Holt also mention several characteristics identifying the individual who is particularly vulnerable to disassociation: immature ego development, unstable, fragile defense mechanism, non-flexible defense structure and generally low ego autonomy.

THE EFFECTS OF DISASSOCIATION

Discomfort of one sort or another, resulting either in personality destruction or construction (or both), is the general effect on people. Specific effects tend to be those for which you are looking, a remark to be kept in mind in reviewing the following analyses.

Goldberger and Holt, using sensory deprivation and isolation, have listed the following effects but caution that they do not occur uniformly: fantasy with direct drive content—often accompanied by anxiety, an increase in vividness of visual and auditory imagery, disturbance of time sense, depersonalization, body image disturbances, feeling of helplessness and inability to modulate mounting drive-tensions. Chambers and Fried report anxiety, oppression, hallucination, illusory experience and fantasy, irritableness, schizoid tendencies and various perceptual difficulties. Schultz adds his observation: ". . . their voices took on a hesitant, drawling quality and they often seemed disoriented and reported feeling confused." He also lists: paranoia, measurable changes in activation levels, disturbances in perception, cognition and learning, a lowering of sensory

What is also clear is that the more a person's continuity with his self and his past is disrupted the less likely is he going to be able to cling to it. Sensory deprivation, isolation and other disassociative influences seem to set the stage for deep personal change. Furthermore, it is increasingly difficult for the subject to be the agent of his change. Schultz remarks that under stimulus deprivation variation of stimuli will have reinforcing properties.

Thus we are brought to the whole new topic of cases, uses and applications. Rapaport gets quite specific when he mentions some examples of interference with the ego's autonomy from the environment, e.g., catatonic conditions of *echopraxia, echolalia,* and *cerea flexibilita;* brainwashing and Nazi mass psychology. However, destruction of the ego's defense mechanisms need not be involuntary. There are situations when a person may purposely seek it, such as in **marathon psychotherapy. The traditional posture in analysis, lying down and looking at the ceiling with the analyst's voice disembodied, is done purposely to keep associating elements out of the analysand's mental landscape.** Other examples are drug or meditation induced states of mystical experience. "Letting go" under these circumstances, is an extremely anxious situation and represents a passage from security of self to extreme vulnerability and loss of identity. The disassociated person's energies are then totally directed toward associating the self to the situation in any way in order to keep together. The tendency to regress (live in the past) in this situation is proof that a person's past experience, if clung to, is a primary force behind continuity of self and the prime inhibitor of change. Often, in marathon therapy, the group leader will insist that references to the past be squelched and life be led in the immediate present as much as possible, for exactly these reasons.

THE CHARACTER OF DISASSOCIATING ELEMENTS

It ought to be mentioned that there are many different *kinds* of disassociation, such as epiphanous, environmental, event caused, disease caused, etc. It also ought to be mentioned, as is already obvious, that the emphasis in this discussion is on environmental disassociation.

As Schultz says, with some labor, "Sensoristasis can be defined as a drive state of cortical arousal which impels the organism to strive to maintain an optimal level of sensory variation." Brownfield quotes Christopher Burney (eighteen months in solitary confinement in prison camp) as saying "Variety is the very stuff of life. We need the constant ebb and flow of sensations, thought, perception, action and emotion." Yarrow and Anderson are just two people who have expressed concern about the consequences of the lack of "richness" in the environments provided for children and the elderly alike. Sonnenfeld, Lee, Kates, Wohlwill are others interested in environmental stimulation. Sensory deprivation and isolation have much broader implications than the "Black Box" or the McGill isolation rooms allow; the effects are not as pronounced but over longer periods of time are just as destructive in their subtler forms. The causes of disassociation have from the start been closely linked to reduced sensory input of all kinds.

Chambers and Fried list the following as inducers of what is termed here as disassociation: isolation, confinement, sensory overload, nongratification of human needs, interference, zero gravity (their study is with respect to space travel), monotony, stress, the symbolic meaning of space (in that situation), physical distance, cultural distance, separation from familiar surroundings, marked changes in sensory input, etc. Ruff, by himself again, says that "Another problem . . . is the occurrence of unaccustomed information input. Even when no physical stressors or threatening implications are involved, subjects may be unable to function properly when novel information is presented." He also shows the difficulty of the task when he says "It would be impossible to catalog all the aspects of an environment that might symbolically threaten any individual." Besides sensory deprivation there is the other side of the coin, sensory overload, ". . . less commonly encountered perhaps and certainly less commonly dealt with experimentally. It implies that two or more sensory modalities are in action simultaneously at levels of intensity greater than normal, and the combination of stimuli is usually introduced suddenly (Lindsley). An example given by Chambers and Fried, from their research in space travel, is the contrast between the sensory deprivation of empty space and the sudden sensory overload of the entire earth coming into the view of the astronaut. A more popular example is the rock concert light show. Cinematic examples include the lighting effects at the end of "Space Odyssey: 2001" and the torture scene in "The Ipcress File."

Moller gets specific about disassociating environments when he quotes Humphry Osmond's writing: "Ambiguous spaces where size, shape, extent and purposes are not clear produce feelings of insecurity and even of panic among those unfamiliar with them." Moller elaborates:

> "It must be emphasized that we are not speaking here of fleeting responses to merely visual perceptions, or of the ability of architecture to evoke an evanescent 'mood,' but of a sustained response to the total complex phenomenon of architectural spaces, which, experienced throughout a sufficient duration of time, will inevitably condition one's emotional states."

Ambiguity, mystery and the inability to identify threatening elements deepen the disassociative experience. Unseen monsters are invariably the worst. The French phrases *déjà vu* (seen before) and *presque vu* (almost seen) can carry this import as part of their meaning.

A great deal more of the characteristics of disassociating elements will come to light when examples are discussed but several things can be said now in general. Elements or environments that have low association values for the subject tend to disassociate; that is to say, there is little in the subject's background or experience with which to *inform* the situation. The charm and security of natural wood and vandalized desk tops is that their history is apparent, they offer their own associations. Sim Van der Ryn's work on this topic points out the importance of imprintability to human beings. If the perceiver can associate the environment with other human beings through their marks of passage he can associate himself to the environment also. "Kilroy" has made many a strange bathroom an immediately familiar place.

Environments which offer no clues as to their ultimate nature—which have no readability—are disassociating. Plastics, porcelain enamel, smooth seamless highly reflective surfaces—are disassociating because they do not provide, by themselves, any clues as to what material they are made of, and how. As always, this is dependent on the experimental resources that individuals can bring to bear. An injection mold process engineer is not likely to be disassociated by such materials while an Eskimo almost certainly will.

Part of the function of readability is lighting, and as suspected, lighting has a great deal to do with whether or not an environment is to be disassociating. The sensory deprivation experiments have used total darkness and non-patterned lighting to great effect. The key effect is to make the environment non-discriminating. We accomplish that in architecture with totally diffuse fluorescent fixtures. Other techniques are over-illumination and under-illumination, both of which raise discrimination thresholds of both form and color. This is particularly effective when the wavelength spectrum moves away from the associating spectrum of natural sunlight, as do certain fluorescent and mercury luminaires. Glare is very effective. For color we have monochrome, for sound we have monotone, for events and form we have monotony; the root being "mono-" or oneness—and it is impossible to discriminate unity.

Highly reflective surfaces, over-bright diffused area (rather than task) lighting. Synthetic materials, bland colors, monotonous rhythms, lonely enclosures. Exactly the sort of disassociative architecture freshmen, away from home for the first time, do not need.

As for dynamic characteristics, elements of environments may be associative or neutral by themselves but not in sequence. This gives cinema an advantage over still-photography for its repertoire of disassociating effects. Surreal sequencing,—for instance, in Buñuel and Dali's "Le Chien Andalu" (1928) can make a movie a very disassociating event to witness. Perhaps a refinement of disassociating sequencing is "fast-cutting," a kind of visual lacuna or enthymeme, where events move unexplainably fast, leaving out parts necessary to their understanding. Over- and under-exposure are similar techniques.

Another important factor in disassociation is framing or context. A disassociating environment, for instance, will lose a great deal of its impact if it has a hole through which one can perceive an associating environment. Similarly, a picture of a disassociating environment is not going to have the power of the presence of the environment itself. With a picture the beholder is always in control. At his discretion he may look away, rip it up or simply not believe it. Frames are effective by degree as well as kind. A photograph held at arm's length will not have the power to disassociate as the image will if it fills the cone of vision completely. A cinematic example is Carol Reed's "The Third Man," where the angle of the camera is always askew of the horizon.

126   With regard to territoriality as a reinforcer of self, lack of defensive capability through area shape, blindness or whatever reason, reduces the subject's sense of security and makes him more susceptible to disassociation. A subset of territoriality, aediculae ("cozy" spaces inside larger spaces), follows the same characteristics. Generally, aediculae, tend to be associating because of their formal reference to the human body (via reference to architecture) and because of their defensive capabilities. The formal reference to the human body is an interesting and relevant feature. Generally, if an environment has obvious accordance with the human body, either stationary or in motion, it will have a high association value.

        A final aspect of disassociative mechanism is teleological in nature. The degree to which an environment is rational, purposeful, and non-contradictory in nature is the degree to which it will be associating. *Non-sequitur* qualities; events and environments which promise a contradiction with past experience or threaten existing structures of order and coherence will always be disassociating until they are explained away. Unpreparedness for an experience that is very unreasonable is very disassociating. To repeat, everyone tends to structure his behavior according to certain expectations about the kind of events one is used to. Severely blunting these expectations produces disassociation on a scale according to how central the expectations are.

What must also be apparent, besides the double-edge characteristic, is the fact that we are all somewhere on a scale ranging from a state of complete association and security (or lack of disassociation) to a state of total insecurity and vulnerability (total disassociation). What makes the sword cut either way: at what point does the disassociative experience stop stimulating and start crippling? Once a person's ego structure is completely destroyed, how does one go about reintegrating the personality into a stronger, more self-reliant and less self-destructive one? These are all questions for further investigation but certain ideas can be tested out loud at this point.

There seem to be certain clear implications for education, for instance. If a student is fed consistent cumulative information his growth in knowledge will be linear and predictable but if he is presented with conflicting, seemingly irreconcilable pictures a certain amount of disassociation will result. If this proves surmountable a different kind of education will occur beyond accrual of dependable information. It is, of course, much more complex to analyze, but salient features are sure to include not only a quantum jump in the understanding of the *context* of the problems at hand but also a more secure and self-reliant student, one willing, then, to take even greater risks. It becomes clear, at least to

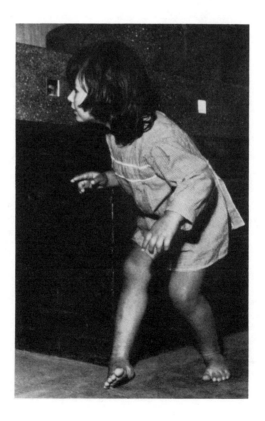

The orphanage in Amsterdam by Aldo van Eyck, c. 1960. Associating devices abound in this institution: morphological references suggesting games or seating postures, scooped-out hollows in exterior aprons to collect reflecting rainwater, tiny mirrors in counter fascia at the eye level of tots, etc. Orphans are exactly a people that need such devices.

this author, that a *certain* amount of disassociation is required for almost *any* kind of "growth," whether personal, educational or environmental.

Internal corridor of a residential dormitory at the University of California at Berkeley. Reflective surfaces without any detail or moulding. The picture looks the same upside down. From Sim van der Ryn's *Dorms at Berkeley*, with permission.

Disassociation, like guns, chewing gum and religion is not ethically functional until the use is specified and the consequences determined. In the case of brainwashing, for instance, one cannot properly say that disassociative processes are "bad." On the contrary, they're just right. The real question is—is brainwashing bad? Situations willfully undertaken, such as psychotherapy, marathon therapy, hypnotism, the transcendental mystical experience, are a different sort of thing. Inasmuch as disassociation can be shown to reinforce these activities the spaces provided ought to be disassociating. Not to do so isn't exactly unethical but it is, indeed, stupid.

Architecture ought to support those activities it is intended for. On the other hand, providing disassociating environments where they are clearly not called for *is* more than stupid; it is immoral. A dormitory for freshmen—people undergoing rapid and frightening changes in their lives—is an example. A hospital for either the mentally or physically sick—full of people fighting desperately for their health and their minds, often suffering from disassociating paranoia and perception distortion—require associating environments that constantly offer reality checks. Urban human service centers which deal with the more vulnerable sectors of our society—the unemployable, the alcoholic, the welfare recipient, the lost and the hopeless—absolutely require the security engendered by associating environments. Ethical issues become clearer when it is realized that parts of our population are more easily disassociated than others. We can control them, if we wish, by providing our institutions that deal with them with disassociating architecture.

The architect, the planner, all environmental designers must be aware of the threshold of disassociation of the people for whom they are designing. The environments ought to be disassociating enough and in such ways as to foster the personal and spatial growth of the users. They should not be disassociative to the point that they undermine the users' self-confidence to negotiate the environment. They ought not threaten but only challenge (if appropriate). The difference is subtle but clear and it differs for different sets of people.

One difficulty is that it is very hard to disassociate the designer, himself, on purely environmental grounds because of his sophistication in this area. The other aspect that makes him invulnerable to his spaces' capacity to disassociate is that he designed it himself; there is nothing mysterious or of unclear purpose to him. Materials that may disassociate others are very associating to him; he knows them intimately—what they're made of, how they fit together and function.

The hazard lies in the fact that the designer has the capacity, in fact the inevitable burden, of playing with peoples' minds. People are always somewhere on a spectrum of association/disassociation and the built environment plays an important part in placing them on that spectrum. If the designer doesn't know the expectations and thresholds of his users with respect to disassociation—or doesn't care—then he is a potentially dangerous member of society. On the other hand, if he is capable of modulating the disassociative capacities of the environment so as to provide simultaneous security and ego stability along with challenge and growth in environmental negotiability then he is providing a great service, indeed.

REFERENCES

Anderson, J.E., Environment and Meaningful Activity" in R.H. Williams et al. (ed) *Processes of Aging: Social and Psychological Perspectives,* Vol. I, N.Y.: Atherton Press, 1963.

Brownfield, C.A., *Isolation,* N.Y.: Random House, 1965.

Chambers, R.M. and Fried, R., "Psychological Aspects of Space Flight," in J.H.W. Brown (ed), *Physiology of Man in Space,* N.Y. Academic Press, 1963.

Goldberger, L. and Holt, R.R., "Experimental Interference with Reality Contact: Individual Differences," in P. Soloman et al. (ed) *Sensory Deprivation,* Cambridge: Harvard University Press, 1961.

Hale, H.B., "The Natural Environment and the Environment of Flight" in S.B. Sells and C.A. Berry (ed), *Human Factors in Jet and Space Age Travel,* N.Y.: Ronald Press, 1961.

Hall, E.T., *The Silent Language,* Greenwich, Conn: Fawcett, 1959.

Kates, R.W., "Stimulus and Symbol: The View of the Bridge," *Journal of Social Issues,* 1966, 4, 21-29.

Kierkegaard, S., *The Journals of Kierkegaard,* N.Y.: Harper and Bros., 1958.

Lee, D.H.K., "The Role of Attitude in Response to Environmental Stress," *Journal of Social Issues,* 1966, 4, 83-92.

Lindsley, D.B., "Common Factors in Sensory Deprivation, Sensory Distortion and Sensory Overload,: in P. Solomon et al. (ed) *Sensory Deprivation,* Cambridge: Harvard University Press, 1961.

Maslow, A.H., "Isomorphic Interrelationships Between Knower and Known," in G. Kepes (ed) *Sign, Symbol, Image,* N.Y.: George Braziller, 1966.

Moller, C.B., *Architectural Environment And Our Mental Health,* N.Y.: Horizon Press, 1968.

Rapaport, D., "The Theory of Ego Autonomy: A Generalization," *Bulletin of the Menninger Clinic,* 1958, 1, 13-35.

Ruff, G.E., "Psychological and Psychophysiological Indices of Stress," in N.M. Burns et al. (ed) *Unusual Environments and Human Behavior,* Glencoe: Free Press of Glencoe, 1963.

Ruff, G.E., Levy, E.Z., and Thaler, V.H., "Factors Influencing Reactions to Reduced Sensory Input" in P. Solomon et al. (ed), *Sensory Deprivation,* Cambridge: Harvard University Press, 1961.

Schultz, D.B., *Sensory Restriction: Effects on Behavior,* N.Y.: Academic Press, 1965.

Sommer, R., *Personal Space: The Behavioral Basis of Design,* Englewood Cliffs, N.J.: Prentice-Hall, 1969.

Sonnenfield, J., "Variable Values in Space Landscape: An Inquiry into the Nature of Environmental Necessity," *Journal of Social Issues,* 1966, 4, 71-83.

Van der Ryn, S., "Architecture, Institutions and Social Change," unpublished paper, 1968.

Wohlwill, J.F., "The Physical Environment: A Problem for a Psychology of

132   Stimulation," *Journal of Social Issues,* 1966, 4, 29-39.

Yarrow, M.F., "Appraising Environment" in R.H. Williams (ed), *Process of Aging: Social and Psychological Perspectives, Vol. I,* N.Y.: Atherton Press, 1963.

Abramovitz, Max 4
The Academies of Art, Past and Present. Cambridge (UK), 1940. See Nikolaus Pevsner.
Accademia del Disigno 55, 73, 74
Ackoff, Russell L. 37, 40
Acorn Structures, Inc. 89
"Adolph Loos", in (reference lost, but c. 1964). See Nikolaus Pevsner.
"Adolph Loos: Ornament and Crime," (reference lost). See Reynor Banham.
Aerospace 36
Aicher, Otl 76
Air Force (U.S.) 36
Air Force (U.S.) Institute of Pathology 53
Alberti, Leon Battista 75
Alcotts (the family) 101
Alexander, Christopher 65, 84, 85, 86
Allen, Gerald 6
Allgemeine Psychiatrie. München, 1913. See Karl Jaspers.
Altman, Irwin 77
Ambasz, Emilio 21
AAAS (American Association for the Advancement of Science) 39, 44, 78
AIA (American Institute of Architects) 6, 85
American Psychological Association 78
American Scholar (journal) 31
American Sociological Association 78
American Space. New York City, 1972. See J. B. Jackson.
AT & T (American Telephone and Telegraph) 55
American University 57
America's Technology Slip. New York City, 1980. See Simon Ramo.
Anatomy of Architecture. New York City, 1979. See George Mansell.
Anderson, J. E. 123
ANSER 36
l'Antiquaire. Paris, 1954. See Henri Bosco.
Antonioni, Michelangelo 114
The Anxiety of Influence. New York City and Oxford, 1973. See Harold Bloom.
Archea, John 77
Archer, L. Bruce 77
The Architect. New York City and Oxford, 1976. See Spiro Kostof.
De Architectura. New York City,

1931. See Pollio Vitruvius.
Architectural Design (magazine), London. 5
Architectural Digest (magazine), Los Angeles. 88
Architectural Judgment. Montreal, 1971. See Peter Collins.
Architectural Record (magazine), New York City. 49, 88
Architectural Psychology Newsletter (now *Man-Environment Systems* [M-ES]). 77
Architecture and Its Interpretation. New York City, 1979. See Juan Pablo Bonta.
The Architecture of Ludwig Wittgenstein. New York City and Halifax, 1976. See Bernard Leitner.
Architecture and the Spirit of Man. Cambridge (MA), 1949. See Joseph Hudnut.
Architecture Research and Teaching (now *Journal of Architectural and Planning Research*) 78
Aristotle 3, 30, 100
Armstrong, Louis 114
Armstrong, William 96
Army (U.S.) 36
Army (U.S.) Corps of Engineers 61
Arnheim, Rudolf 42, 78
Art as Experience. New York City, 1934. See John Dewey.
Arthur D. Little 36
Asimow, Morris 76
Aspects of Scientific Explanation. New York City, 1965. See Carl Hempel.
ACSA (Association of Collegiate Schools of Architecture) 4
Association for the Study of Man-Environment Relations (ASMER) 5, 78
Association Philotechnique 34
Auden, W. H. 26
Augustine, Saint 69
Austen, Jane 100
Ayer, Alfred Jules 29, 31, 65, 99

Bachelard, Gaston 90, 91
Bacon, Francis 44
Bailey, Roger 77
Bakelite 12, 13
Balzac, Honoré de 34
Banham, Raynor 67
Bannister, Turpin C. 67
Bargate, Simon 5
Barton, Russell 76
Bateson, Gregory 27, 63

Bauhaus (school of architecture) 12, 19, 67, 68, 76
Beinart, Julian 89
Bergson, Henri 102
Bernal, J. D. 35
Bertalanffy, Ludwig von 29, 39, 40, 78
Bechtel, Robert 77
Biasatti, Angel 5
BIC. See Baron Bich.
Bich, Baron 12
Bierman, Harold 35
"Big Mac". See Ray Kroc.
Birdseye, Clarence 56
Bismark, Prince Otto von 47
Black, Max 31
Blackett, Patrick M. S. 35
Blake, William 88
Bloom, Harold 19
"Blow-Up" (film). See M. Antonioni.
Bohnert, H. 36
Boldyreff, Alex 38
Bonaparte, Napoleon 33, 47
Bonta, Juan Pablo 78, 99
"Boot Strap Essence-Seeking," JAE (*Journal of Architectural Education*), Vol. XXIX, No. 2 (November, 1975). See Robert Harris.
Booth, George 103, 104
Boretsky, Michael 60
Bosco, Henri 97
BOSTI. See Buffalo Organization for Social and Technological Innovation, Inc.
Boudon, Philippe 72
Boulding, Kenneth E. 5, 39, 58
Breuer, Marcel 4
Bridgman, Percy W. 29, 44, 63
Brill, Michael 80, 81
Broadbent, Geoffrey 76, 78, 84
Bronowski, Jacob 31, 35, 37, 40, 42
Brookhaven (National Laboratory) 47
Brown, Robert 59
Brownfield, C. A. 123
Buffalo Organization for Social and Technological Innovation, Inc. 80, 81
The Builders. New York City, 1978. See Martin Mayer.
Bulgarian Cultural Institute 65
Bunshaft, Gordon 81
Buñuel, Luis 125
Buonarroti, Michaelangelo 73, 74
Burney, Christopher 123
Buscoviach, Roger Joseph 75
Bush, Vannevar 34, 36, 45
Byron, Lord George Gordon 26

134

Cadillac (car) 24
California Polytechnic/San Luis Obispo 77
Callicrates 85
Camus, Albert 33
Canter, David 79, 80, 99
Carlo, Gian Carlo de 89
Carnap, Rudolph 29, 30, 31, 32, 36
Carnegie-Mellon University 50
Carnot, Lazare 33
Carroll, Lewis 119
Carson, Pirie, & Scott 70, 71
Carson, Rachel 87
Case Western Reserve University 37, 76
Center for Disease Control 53
Chambers, R. M. 122, 123, 124
Charles the Bold, King 44
Cheever, John 4, 7
Cheval, le Facteur 105
"le Chien Andalu" (film) See Buñeul or Dali
Choisey, Auguste 69
Churchill, Winston 11
Churchman, Charles West 37
City College of the City University of New York 6
"Civilizing Education: Uniting Liberal and Professional Learning," in *Daedalus*, Vol. 103, No. 4 (Fall 1974). See Martin Meyerson.
Clarke, David 4
Cleveland, Grover 71
Coast Guard (U.S.) 60
Cohen, Sidney 77
Collins, Peter 89
Complicity and Conviction. Cambridge (MA), 1980. See William Hubbard.
Comte, Auguste 29, 33, 34, 75
"Concealed Rhetoric in Scientist's Scociology", in *Scientism and Values*, Helmut Schock, Editor. Princeton, 1960. See Richard Weaver.
"The Conceptual Framework of Psychology" by Egon Brunswik, in *Foundations of the Unity of Science*, edited by Otto Neurath, et al. Chicago, 1938.
Concrete (journal) 65
CBO (Congressional Budget Office) 38
Conjectures and Reputations. New York City, 1962. See Karl Popper.
Cooper, Clare C. 79, 80
Le Corbusier. See Charles Jeanneret-Gris.
Cornell University 38
"Cosmology", by E. Findlay-

Freundlich, in *Foundations in the Unity of Science*, edited by Otto Neurath, et al. Chicago, 1938.
The Counter-Revolution of Science. Glencoe, 1955. See F. A. von Hayek.
Cousins, Norman 53
Cours de Philosophie Positive. Paris, 1908. See Auguste Comte.
Craik, Kenneth 76
Cranbrook Academy 6, 102-109
Cratchit, Bob 22
Cybernetics. New York City, 1948. See Norbert Wiener.
Cycenas, Frank 6

DADA 89
Daedalus (journal) 88
Daedalus, Stephen 98
Dali, Salvador 125
Dalkey, Norman 36
Dallas-Fort Worth Airport 16, 18
Danzig, George 37
Dartmouth University 39
Darwin, Charles 29
Davidson, Sidney 36
Da Vinci, Leonardo 46
Debs, Eugene 71
Delphi (technique) 36
Democritus 41
Denbitz, L. M. 35
Department of Commerce 60
Department of Defense 45, 56, 62, 122
Department of Energy 46
Department of Labor Office of Productivity and Technology 59
Design in Architecture. London, 1973. See Geoffrey Broadbent.
Design: A Case History; A Designer's Specification for a Computer System. Cambridge (MA), 1967. See John Myer.
Design of Cities. See Edmund Bacon.
D.M.G. (Design Methods Group) *Newsletter* (now *Design Theories and Methods*). 76, 77
Design Methods in Architecture Symposium. New York City, 1969. See Geoffrey Broadbent or Anthony Ward (Editors).
Design Theories & Methods (journal), San Luis Obispo.
Design Research Society 76, 77
Design Studies (journal) 77
Design Theories and Methods (journal) 76
"Design Training", in *How It Works*, D. Clarke (Editor). London, 1977. See David Clarke.

"The Development and Structure of the Biomedical Literature", in *Coping with the Biomedical Literature*. A primer for the Scientist and the Clinician, Kenneth S. Warren, Editor, New York City, 1981. See Derek Price.
Dexis, A Feasibility Study. Proprietory to Mead Data Control. New York City, 1980. See David Clarke.
Dewey, John 73
Doblin, Jay 23
Documents d'Architecture Modern (lithograph series). Paris, early in this century.
Douglas, Donald 36
Doxiades, Konstantine 75
Dresch, Stephen 5, 56, 58
Drexler, Arthur 31
Drucker, Peter F. 61, frontispiece
Dubislav, Walter 39
Dulles Airport 17, 18

Easter Hill Village. New York City, 1975. See Clare Cooper.
Eberhard, John 76, 80
Eccentric Spaces. New York City, 1977. See Robert Harbison.
Ecole des beaux-arts (school of architecture) 17
Ecology of Knowledge Group 5
Ecole polytechnique (school of engineering) 33, 34
Ecole des ponts et chaussés (school of bridges and roads) 34
The Economic Consequences of the Peace. New York City, 1925. See J. M. Keynes.
Edison, Thomas Alva 57
Either/Or. Princeton, 1971. See Søren Kierkegaard.
E.D.R.A. See Environmental Design and Research Association.
Einstein, Albert 29, 40, 44, 46, 63, 64
Eisenhower, Dwight David 36, 45, 68, 70
Eisenman, Peter 21, 74, 105
Ekistics. London, 1968. See Konstantine Doxiades.
Eliot, Thomas Stearns 87
Emerson, Ralph W. 121
Emery, F. E. 61
Emmanuel II, Victor (Emmanuelle, Vittorio) 84, 107, 108
Engelmann, Paul 65, 67
Engineering-News Record 61
Engineering Our Future. London,

1980. See Sir Montigue Finniston.

English, David 5

Environment and Behavior (E&B) (journal), Beverly Hills. 77

Environmental Design and Research Association 77, 78

Erkenntis (now *Journal of Unified Science*) 30

Essays in Science. New York City, 1955. See Albert Einstein.

Esser, Aristide 5, 78

Etc: A Review of General Semantics. Current whereabouts unknown. 40

Experiencing Architecture. Cambridge (MA), 1970. See Steen E. Rasmussen.

Explorations in Meaning of Architecture. Woodstock (NY), 1979. See Suzanne H. Crowhurst Lennard.

Eyck, Aldo van. See *Team 10 Primer.* 5, 75, 106, 107, 126-127

"Facts and Models" in *Design Methods in Architecture,* Geoffrey Broadbent & Anthony Ward, Editors. New York City, 1969. See Amos Rapoport.

Far From the Madding Crowd. New York City, 1984. See Thomas Hardy.

Farnsworth, Dr. 2

Federal Reserve Board 38

Feigl, Herbert 29, 31

Ficino, Marsilio 75

"The Fight For Clarity: Logical Positivism", in *American Scholar,* Vol. 8, No. 1 (Winter 1938-39). See Ernest Nagel.

Filarete, Antonio 75

Fisher, R. B. 35

Flagle, Charles 37, 38

Flexner Report (AMA) 53

The Fly in the Amber. Author published, 1957. See Ralph Walker.

Ford Foundation 36, 79

Ford, Henry 56, 85, 86

Ford Motor Company 62, 63

Fores, Michael 48

"Forword" to *Science and the Goals of Man* by Anatol Rapoport, New York City, 1950. See S. I. Hayakawa.

Fortune (magazine) 60

"Foundations of Biology" by Felix Mainx, in *Foundations of the Unity of Science,* edited by Otto Neurath, et al. Chicago, 1938.

Foundations of the Unity of Science, two volumes. Chicago, 1955. See Otto Neurath, et al., Editors. Note: this was to be the start of an *International Encyclopedia of Unified Sciences* of which only these two volumes were realized.

Frank, Philip 29, 31

Frege, Gottlob 65

Fried, R. 122, 123, 124

From Bauhaus To Our House. New York City, 1981. See Thomas Wolfe.

Fuller, Buckminister 75

Galilei, Galileo 46

Galileo. See G. Galilei.

"Games, Decisions and Organizations," *General Systems Yearbook, 1959.* Ann Arbor, 1959. See Russell Ackoff.

Gans, Herbert 76

Gantt, Henry 34

Gargoyle (literary magazine) 5

General System Theory. New York City, 1968. See Ludwig von Bertalanffy.

General Systems (yearbooks) 39

Gerard, Ralph 39

Gersellschaft Für Empirische Philosophie 39

Gestalt Psychology. New York City, 1929. See Wolfgang Köhler.

Geymuller, ? 69

Gibbs, Willard 32

Gibson, Ralph E. 37, 38

Giedion, Sigfried 75

Glacken, Clarence 74

Gödel (Goedel), Kurt 29, 30, 31, 34, 42

Goldberger, L. 119, 120, 122

Goodhue, Bertram 107

Gorki, Maxim 103

Grant, Donald P. 77

The Great Chain of Being. Cambridge (MA), 1961. See Arthur Lovejoy.

Greenberg, Daniel S. 44, 46

Grieg, Edvard 103

Gropius, Walter 12, 67, 89

Guarini, Guarino 75

Habitat. See Moshe Safdie.

Hadrians Memoirs. New York City, 1954. See Marguerite Yourcenar.

Hahn, Hans 29, 31, 40

Haiger, Ernst (of the architecture firm of Helbig & Haiger) 104

Hale, M. B. 121

Hall, Edward T. 75, 121

Hamlyn Group 5

Handler, Philip 46

Hans (no surname permitted) 91, 94, 96, 102

Harbison, Robert 90

Hardy, Thomas 4, 69, 70

Harries, Karsten 27

Harris, Robert 25, 50

Harvard University 119

Hawthorne, Nathaniel 101

Hayakawa, S. I. 40, 43

Hayek, Friedrich August von 33

Head, Howard 56, 70, 71

Healy, Tim 5

Hejduk, John 74

Hegel, G. W. F. 100

Heidegger, Martin 23

Heifetz, Jascha 49

Heisenberg, Werner 29

Helmer, Olaf 36

Helmuth, Obata & Kassabaum (architecture firm) 18

Helmuth, Yamasaki & Leinweber (architecture firm) 72, 73

Hempel, Carl Gustav 29, 30, 39

Hersey, George L. 69

Herzberg, Alex 39

Hesse, Herman 4

Heydenreich, ? 69

The Hidden Dimension. Garden City, 1966. See E. T. Hall.

Higgins, William 37

History of Western Philosophy. New York City, 1945. See Bertrand Russell.

Hitler, Adolf 12

Hochschule Für Gestaltung 76

Hodgkinson, Harold 54

Holiday Inn University 54

Holt, R. R. 119, 120, 122

Hoover, Herbert 45, 56

House & Garden (magazine), New York City. 88

Hubbard, William 1

Hudnut, Joseph 24

Hugo, Victor 4, 115

The Hunchback of Notre Dame. Roslyn (New York), c. 1928. See Victor Hugo.

Human Action. New Haven, 1949. See Ludwig von Mises.

Human Factors Society 78

The Human Use of Human Beings: Cybernetics and Society. Garden City, 1954. See Norbert Wiener.

Hummro 36

Husserl, Edmund 32

Ictinus 85

Ibsen, Henrik 103

Ideas. London, 1952. See Edmund Husserl.

The Identity of Man. Garden City,

136

1971. See Jacob Bronowski.
The Image of the Architect. New Haven, 1983. See Andrew Saint.
International Institute for Applied Systems Analysis 69
Institutional Neuroses. Bristol, 1966. See Russell Barton.
International Encyclopedia of Unified Science. See *Foundations of the Unity of Sciences.*
The Interpretation of Ordinary Landscapes. New York City and Oxford, 1979. See D. W. Meinig (Editor).
Introduction to Design. Englewood Cliffs, 1962. See Morris Asimow.
Inquiry By Design. Monterey, 1981. See John Zeisel.
IBM (International Business Machines) 61, 81-83
L'Isle, Villiers de
International Association for the Study of People and their Physical Surroundings (IAPS) 78
"The Ipcress File" (film) 124
Iron Guard 7
Irving, Washington 101
Isuzu (car manufacturer) 60
Ittelson, William 76, 77

Jackson, John Brinkerhoff 5, 89, 90
Jacobs, Jane 87
Jaspers, Karl 28, 32
Jeanneret-Gris, Charles E. (Le Corbusier). 37, 67, 72, 88
Jeffers, Robinson 101
Jefferson, Thomas 75
Jencks, Charles 20, 106
Jobs, Steven 56
Johnston, William M. 30
John the Scot 44
Johns Hopkins University 37
Johnson, Lyndon B. 62
Johnson, Philip
Johnston, William M. 30
Jones, Christopher 77
Jones, Inigo 12
JAE (Journal of Architectural Education) 4
Journal of Architectural and Planning Research. Arlington (Texas). 78
Journal of Architectural Psychology. New York City and London. 78
Journal of Architectural Research (now *Journal of Architectural and Planning Research*) 78
Journal of Environmental Psychology. London. 78
Journal of Unified Science. Current

whereabouts unknown. 30
Journal Social Issues, Vol. 22 (1966). See R. W. Kates & J. F. Wohlwill (Editors). 76
Jowett, Benjamin 48
Jukos (Juhos), Béla von 29
Jung, Carl G. 92, 93, 94, 96

Kahn, Louis 88
Kaila, E. 29
Kaiser, Wilhelm 47
Kammerer, Marcellus 104
Kaplan, Abraham 36
Kates, R. W. 76, 123
Kaufman, Henry 7, 38
Kaufmann, Felix 29, 31
Kaysen, Carl 88
Kepler, Johannes 41
Keynes, Lord John Maynard 28, 63
Kierkegaard, Søren 27, 120
Kilgore, Harley 45
Kimball, George 35, 36, 37
Kindergarten Chats. New York City, 1947. See Louis Sullivan.
Kleinsasser, William, frontispiece
Köhler, Wolfgang 39, 78
Kostof, Spiro K. 70
Kraft, Victor 29
Kramer, Hilton 107
Krauss, Richard 51
Kretschmann, Klaus 5
Kroc, Ray 12
Krüeger 5, 21
Kuhn, Thomas S. 19, 31
Kurtz, Stephen A. 104

Laing, R. D. 100
Landscape (journal). Berkeley. 90
Landscapes. Amherst (MA), 1970. See J. B. Jackson.
Lee, D. M. K. 123
Leibnitz, Gottfried von 15, 100
Leitner, Bernhard 5, 65
Lennard, Suzanne H. Crowhurst 101
"Letter to Lord Byron" (poem). See W. H. Auden.
Levinson, Horace 35
Levinson, Nanette 51
Levy, E. Z. 120, 122
Lewin, Kurt 39
Life (magazine)
Lincoln, Abraham
Lindemann, F. A. 35
Lindsley, D. B. 124
Linguistic Aspects of Science. See Neurath or Carnap or Morris, C. (Editors).
Linz Café. See Christopher Alexander.
Little, Arthur D.

Lived-in Architecture. Cambridge (MA), 1969. See Philippe Boudon.
Living Systems. New York City, 1978. See James Miller.
Logical Positivism. Glencoe, 1959. See A. J. Ayer (Editor).
Logic of Modern Physics. New York City, 1927. See Percy Bridgman.
The Logic of Scientific Discovery. London, 1968. See Karl Popper.
Loos, Adolph 65, 67, 68, 69, 89
Lorch, Emil 104
Lotz, W. 69
Lovejoy, Arthur O. 42
Lubetkin, Berthold 107
Ludwig Wittgenstein, A Memoir. New York City, 1966. See Norman Malcolm.

Mach, Ernst 29
McNamara, Robert S. 62
Maeterlink, Count Maurice 95
Magister Judi: The Glass Bead Game. New York City, 1964. See Herman Hesse.
Mahler, Gustav 103
Malcolm, Norman 67
Man-Environment Systems (M-ES) (journal). Orangeburg, New York. 77, 78
Mansell, George 5
Maroti, Geza 108
Marshall, John 28, 61, 85
Marshall Cavendish 4
Marx, Karl 28, 100
Maslow, Abraham 121
MIT (Massachusetts Institute of Technology) 37, 59, 75, 89
Massachusetts Institute of Technology Center for Building Research 51
The Mathematical Theory of Communication. Urbana, 1949. See Claude Shannon or Warren Weaver.
Mayer, Martin 72
McDonnell Douglas 36
McGill University 119, 123
McLuhan, Marshall 88
McMillen, Peg (Margaret) 89
McNulty, Robert 89
Mead Corporation 39
Mead Data Control 39, 51
The Meaning of Modern Art Evanston (IL) 1968. See Karsten Harries.
Medici, Cosimo de 55, 73
Men, Ideas and Politics. New York City, 1971. See Peter Drucker.
Mendel, Gregor Johann 29
Mendelsohn, Erich 67

Mendelssohn, J. L. Felix 103
Menger, Karl 29
Menninger Clinic 119
Methodology of Mathematical Economics and Econometrics, by Gerhard Tintner, in *Foundations of the Unity of Science,* edited by Otto Neurath, et al. Chicago, 1939.
Methods of Operations Research. Cambridge (MA), 1951. See Philip Morse or George Kimball.
Methods of Operations Research (book review), *Scientific American,* Vol. 185, No. 4 (Oct 1951). See Jacob Bronowski.
Metternich, Prince Klemens W. N. L. Von 30
Meyerson, Martin 69, 80
Michaelangelo. See M. Buonarroti.
Mies van der Rohe. New York City, 1960. See Arthur Drexler.
Miller, James G. 39
Miller, Arjay 62, 63
Milton, John 95, 97
MITI (Ministry of International Trade and Industry) 60
Mises, Ludwig von 32
Mises, Richard von 34, 40
The Modular. Cambridge (MA), 1968. See Charles Jeanneret-Gris.
Molière, J. B. P. 36
Moller, Clifford B. 124
Monaldo, Tomas 76
Monge, G. 33
Moore, Charles (Chuck) 98
Moore, Gary T. 5, 76, 77
Moore, G. E. 31, 65
Morganstern, Oskar 37, 39
Morrill, Justin Smith (Morrill Act) 48
Morris, Charles W. 31
Morse, Philip M. 35, 36, 37
Moss, Sidney 101
Mozart, Wolfgang A. 92
Muller, Paul 87
Muller-Kaiser Study (AMA) 53
Mulligan, Buck 96, 98
Musée Pompidou (Place Beaubourg) 19, 20
Mustang (car) 24
Myer, John 51
Meyerson, Martin 54
The Myth of Sisyphus. New York City, 1955. See Albert Camus.

Naddor, Eliezar 37
Nagel, Ernest 31, 32, 99
Napoleon. See N. Bonaparte

Napoleon III, Louis 34
NASA (National Aeronautical and Space Administration) 122
National Academy of Science 44
National Academy of Science Advisory Board on Built Environment 76
National Bureau of Standards Center for Building Technology 76, 80
NCARB (National Council of Architectural Registration Boards 75
National Institutes of Health 53
National Institutes of Mental Health 76, 77
National Research Council Commission on Human Resources 64
NSF (National Science Foundation) 5, 45, 48, 56
National Training Laboratories 54
National Trust for Historic Preservation 89
Naval Ordnance Laboratory 37
Navy (U.S.) 36
Neumann, John (Johan) von 37, 39
Neurath, Otto 28, 29, 31, 33, 75, 99
Neutra, Dione 30
Neutra, Richard 30
New School for Social Research 42
New Directions in Psychology 4. New York City, 1970. See Kenneth Craik.
The New Criterion (journal), New York City.
Newman, Cardinal 48
"The New Scientific Thought and its Impact," in Vol. VI, Part One of the UNESCO *History of Mankind.* New York City, 1966. See Jacob Bronowski.
New Yorker (magazine), New York City. 89
Nietzsche, Freidrich W. 28
Nixon, Richard M. 34, 63
Nobel, Alfred 52, 86, 96
Notes on the Synthesis of Form. Cambridge (MA), 1964. See Christopher Alexander.
Novum Organum. London, 1844. See Francis Bacon.

Oeuvres de Saint-Simon et d'Enfantin. Paris, 1865-1878. See Saint-Simon.
Office of Naval Research 45
Ohl, Herbert 76
OPEC (Organization of Petroleum Exporting Countries) 63

Open Aŕk B. V. 21
OEG (Operations Evaluations Group) 36
On Further Examination. College Entrance Examination Board. New York City, 1977.
OAG (Operations Analysis Group) 36
Operations Research. New York City, 1971. See Charles West Churchman.
ORO (Operations Research Office) 36
Operation Research Society 37
Origen (Origenes Adamantius) 68
"Ornament und Verbrechen", in *Adolf Loos* by Ludwig Munz, et al., New York City, 1966. See Adolf Loos.
Orwell, George 4
Osmond, Humphrey 76, 124
Otis (elevator) 56
Owings, Nathaniel 81

Pacioli, Lucca 88
Pasteur, Louis 46
Patrick, Linda 6
A Pattern Language. New York City, 1977. See Christopher Alexander.
Pattison, Mark 48
Pauker, Anna 7
Peace Corps 62
Peña, William 15, 22, 100
Penner, Rudolph 38
Pennsylvania State University 77
Pennsylvania State University Office of Continuing Education 51
The Personal Opinions of Honoré de Balzac. Boston, 1899. See H. Balzac.
Pevsner, Nikolaus 69
"Phases of the Moon" (poem). See W. B. Yeats
Philosophical Foundations of Physics. New York City, 1966. See Rudolf Carnap.
Philosophy in The Twentieth Century. New York City, 1982. See A. J. Ayer.
Piaget, Jean 120
Piano and Rogers (architecture firm) 20
Pierce, Charles 31
Pincus, I. N. 35
Piretti, Giancarlo 21
Place Beaubourg. See Musée Pompidou.
Planck, Max 28, 39
Plato 85, 88, 100

Plath, Sylvia 95
La Poétique de l'Espace (The Poetics of Space). New York City, 1968. See Gaston Bachelard.
The Politics Of Pure Science. New York City, 1968. See Daniel Greenberg.
Pope, Alexander 101
Popper, Karl R. 28, 31, 40, 41, 46
Portaghesi, Paolo 74
The Portable Nietzche. New York City, 1954. See Friedrich Nietzche.
Portsmouth Polytechnic Institute 76
Positivism Cambridge (UK), 1951. See Richard (not Ludwig) von Mises.
"Postmodern," *New Criterion,* September 1982. See Hilton Kramer.
Price, Derek deSolla, frontispiece, 5, 45, 46, 50, 56
Principia Mathmatica. Cambridge (UK), 1975. See Bertrand Russell or A. N. Whitehead.
"Principles of the Theory of Probability", by Ernest Nagel in *Foundations of the Unity of Science,* edited by Otto Neurath, et al. Chicago, 1938.
Priscus, Neratius 102
Progressive Architecture (magazine). Stamford. 88, 110
Proshansky, Harold M. 76
"Prospect for the 80s: A Study of Soviet-American Education and Technical Development." Unpublished paper, Department of Political Economy, Catholic University, Washington, D.C., 1980. See Robert Brown.
Protzen, Jean-Pierre 77
Pruitt-Igoe (housing project) 72
Psychology for Architects. London, 1974. See David Cantor.
"The Psychopathology of Scientism," in *Scientism and Values,* edited by Helmut Schoeck, Princeton.
Pullman, George 71
(Historic) Pullman Foundation 5
Pythagorean Palaces. Ithaca, 1976. See G. L. Hersey.

Quantitative Analysis for Business Decisions. Homewood (IL), 1977. See Harold Bierman, et al.
"Quantitative Analysis and National Security," in *World Politics,* Vol. XX, No. 2 (January

1963). See James Schlesinger.
Quinn, Patrick 97, 98

Ramo, Simon 55
RAC 36
RAND Corporation 36, 61, 62
The Rand Corporation. Cambridge (MA), 1966. See Bruce Smith.
Rapaport, David 119, 120, 123
Rapaport, Anatol 37, 39, 40, 42, 43
Rapoport, Amos 84
Rasmussen, Steen Eiler 99, 111
The Rationalists. New York City, 1978. See Dennis Sharp.
Reagan, Ronald 56, 57, 76
"The Recognition of Systems Engineering," in *Operations Research and Systems Engineering,* edited by Charles Flagle, et al., Baltimore, 1960. See Ralph E. Gibson.
Reed, Carol 125
Reichenbach, Hans 30, 39
Reswick, James 76
Richardson, H. H. 7, 95
Rodilla, Simon 95, 105
Rohe, Ludwig Mies van der 2, 31, 67, 81, 83
Rosenstein, Allen 5
Rossignol Cie. 71
Rudolph, Paul
Ruff, G. E. 120, 122, 124
Russell, Bertrand 28, 31, 40, 65, 68, 112
Ryle, Gilbert 31, 99, 100
Ryn, Sim van der 124, 128

Saarinen, Eero 18, 106
Saarinen, Eliel 2, 86, 92, 95, 96, 103-109, 114
Saarinen, Loja 106
Sacconi, G. 115
Saint, Andrew 67
Saint-Simon, Henri, Comte de 34, 75
Safdie, Moshe 5, 14
Salk, Jonas 44
Sanoff, Henry 77
Santayana, George 100
Schindler, R. M. 30
Schlesinger, James R. 62
Schlick, Moritz 28, 29, 31, 39, 78
SAT (Scholastic Aptitude Test) 61
Schultz, D. B. 122, 123
Schweitzer, Albert 85, 86
Science and The Goals of Man. New York City, 1950. See Anatol Rapoport.
"Science and Industry, Challenges of Antagonistic Interdependence," *Science,* Vol. 204, No. 4395 (25 May 1979).

See Peter Drucker.
Sciences of the Artificial. Cambridge (MA), 1981. See H. A. Simon.
"The Science/Technology Relationship, The Craft of Experimental Science, and Policy For The Improvement of High Technology Innovation." Unpublished 1982 NSF Report. See Derek Price.
Scientific American (magazine) 75
Scott, Michael 96
SDC 36
Selected Essays. New York City, 1932. See T. S. Eliot.
A Series of Plans for Cottages. London, 1781. See John Ward the Younger.
Shakespeare, William 88
Shannon, Claude E. 39, 76
Sharp, Dennis 68
Shelley, Percy B. 95, 97
Sibelius, Jean J. G. 103
Sidel, Andrew 78
Silber, John 89
Simon, Herbert A. 11, 36, 55
Skidmore, Louis 81
Skidmore, Owings & Merrill (architecture firm) 72, 81, 82, 83
Skidmore, Owings, & Merrill. New York City, 1970. See Christopher Woodward.
Smith, Bruce 36
Smith, Kenneth A. 57
Snow, Charles Percy 41, 48
Société Polytechnique 34
Society for General Systems Research 5, 39
Socrates 100, 102
Sonnenfeld, J. 123
SOM. See Skidmore, Owings & Merrill.
Sommer, Robert 22, 76, 112, 121
SIU (Southern Illinois University) School of Medicine 53
SORO 36
"Space Odyssey: 2001" (film) 124
Space and Society (journal). Cambridge (MA) and Milan 89
Space, Time & Architecture. Cambridge (MA), 1949. See Sigfried Giedion.
Spearman, Jerry 5
Spinoza, Baruch 100
SRI 36
Stalin (Stalinize), Joseph 7
Stanford University 37
Stanford University Center for Advanced Studies in Behavorial Science 39
(SUNYAB) State University of

New York at Buffalo 80
Stea, David 76
Stegmann, ? 69
Steps Towards An Ecology Of The Mind. San Francisco, 1972. See Gregory Bateson.
Stevens, Wallace 98
Stockman, David 38
Strindberg, Johan A. 103
Strodtbeck, Fred 23
Structure of Scientific Revolutions. Chicago, 1964. See Thomas Kuhn.
Studer, Ray 76
Su, Yuk Wing 34
Sullivan, Louis Henry 2, 22, 70
Summa Theologica. Cambridge (UK), 1964. See St. Thomas Aquinas.
Swarthmore College 39
"Systems, Organizations, and Interdisciplinary Research," *General Systems Yearbook, 1960.* See Russell Ackoff.
Systems Thinking. Harmondworth, Middlesex, 1969. See F. E. Emery.

Tarski (the Pole) 32, 42
Taylor, Calvin 77
Taylor, Frederick 34, 35
"Teaching Research Isn't Teaching Engineering," in *Engineering Education,* Vol. 68, No. 4 (January 1978). See Eric Walker.
The Ten Books on Architecture. Rome, C. 75 B.C. See P. Vitruvius.
Thaler, V. H. 120, 122
Theories of Logical Positivism. Unpublished, written in 1938. See Max Black.
Theory of Games and Economic Behavior. Princeton, 1947. See John von Neumann or Oskar Morganstern.
Thiel, Philip 5, 77
Thiel, Richard frontispiece
"The Third Man" (film). See Carol Reed.
Thomas, Cathy 4
Thomas (from) Aquinas, Saint 30
Thomas, W. N. 35
"Those Worrisome Technology Experts," by Herbert E. Meyer, *Fortune,* Vol. 97, No. 10 (22 May 1978). See Michael Boretsky.
Through The Looking Glass. London, 1872. See Lewis Carroll.
The Timeless Way of Building. New

York City, 1979. See Christopher Alexander.
Tolstoy, Count Lev N. 65
Topophilia. Englewood Cliffs, 1974. See Yi-Fu Tuan.
"Toward a Model of Science Indicators" in *Toward A Metric Of Science* Yehuda Elkana, et al., Editors, New York City, 1978. See Derek deSolla Price.
Toward A Psychology Of Art. Berkeley, 1966. See R. Arnheim.
"The Tower"; "The Winding Stair" (poems). See W. B. Yeats.
Traces On The Rhodian Shore. Berkeley, 1967. See Clarence Glacken.
Tractatus Logico-philosophicus. London, 1974. See Ludwig Wittgenstein.
Truman, Harry 45
Tuan, Yi-Fu 90
The Two Cultures and the Scientific Revolution. Cambridge (UK), 1959. See C. P. Snow.

Übermensch. See F. Nietzsche.
Ulm School of Design 76
Union Carbide Corporation 87
The Unity of Science. London, 1934. See Rudolf Carnap
University of Alberta 39
University of Arizona 77
University of Berlin 28, 65
University of Bologna 54
UCLA (University of California at Los Angeles) 53
University of California at Berkeley 6, 45, 49, 76, 79
University of California at Berkeley School of Criminology 49
University of Kentucky 6
University of Lancaster 41
University of Liverpool 75
University of Manchester 65
University of Massachusetts 89
University of Michigan 37, 40, 104
University of Michigan Mental Health Research Institute 40
University of North Carolina 77
University of Oregon 6, 125
University of Pennsylvania 41
University of Salerno 54
U.S.C. (University of Southern California) 25, 49
University of Texas/Arlington 78
University of Utah 77
University of Vienna 28, 37
University of Virginia 75
University of Washington 5
University of Wisconsin/Milwaukee 3

Valéry Paul 102
"Value", *Concrete,* Vol. 1 No. 8 (1977). See Christopher Alexander.
Vasari, Giorgio 54, 73, 74, 75
Veterans Administration 53
Ventre, Francis 110
Venturi, Robert 1
Venturi, Vanna
Verein Ernst Mach (The Earnst Mach Society) 29
Vertebra (chair) 5
Vienna Circle. See *Wiener Kreis.*
Vienna, Vienna. New York City, 1980. See William Johnston.
Vinci, Leonardo da 74, 88
La Ville Radieuse. Boulogne, 1935. See Charles Jeanneret-Gris.
Vitruvius, Pollio 74
Volker, Paul 38
Volkswagon (car) 24
Voysey, Charles F. Annesley 104

Waddington, C. H. 35
Waismann, Friedrich 29, 31
Walker, Eric 54
Walker, Ralph 115
Waller, Susan 6
Wall Street Journal (newspaper) 81
Wang, An 54
Wang Institute 54
Ward, Tony 84
Warren, Kenneth S. 5
The Washington Post (newspaper) 54, 61
Wasteland: Building the American Dream. New York City, 1973. See Stephen Kurtz.
Waterman, Alan T. 45
Ways, M. 61
Weaver, Richard M. 33
Weaver, Warren 39, 76
Weinberg, Julius, frontispiece, 5
Werk (magazine). 5
"What Could an Undergraduate Education Do?" in *Daedalus,* Vol. 103, No. 4 (Fall, 1974). See Carl Kaysen.
White, Stanford 7
Whitehead, Alfred North 28, 31, 40
Wiener, Norbert, 34, 35, 37, 39, 40, 75
Wiener Kreis 28, 30, 40, 43, 67, 75
Wilsen, Thomas Woodrow 28
Winkel, Gary 76, 77
Wissenschoftliche Weltauffasung: Der Wiener Kreis (The Scientific World View: the Vienna Circle), pamphlet. Vienna, 1928.
Wittgenstein, Gretl 65

Wittgenstein, Hermine 65
Wittgenstein, Ludwig 5, 28, 31, 34, 40, 65, 67, 69
Wizard of Oz 3
Wohlstetter, Albert 36
Wohlwill, J. F. 76, 123
Wolfe, Thomas 68, 71, 105
Wood the Younger, John 86
Woodward, Christopher 81
World Politics (journal) 62
Wraith, Jeremy (pen name of David Clarke)
Wren, Christopher 75
Wright, George Henrick von 67
Wright, Frank Lloyd 7

Yale University Law School 53
Yarrow, M. F. 123
Yeats, William Butler 93, 94, 95, 96, 97, 103
Yourcenar, Marguerite 102
Yuk Wing, Su 34

Zeisel, John 83, 84, 85
Zimmerman, Richard 57
Zube, Ervin 90
Zuckerman, Solly 35